NEW VANGUARD 228

GERMAN COMMERCE RAIDERS 1914–18

RYAN K. NOPPEN   ILLUSTRATED BY PAUL WRIGHT

First published in Great Britain in 2015 by Osprey Publishing,

PO Box 883, Oxford, OX1 9PL, UK

PO Box 3985, New York, NY 10185-3985, USA

E-mail: info@ospreypublishing.com

Osprey Publishing, part of Bloomsbury Publishing Plc

A CIP catalog record for this book is available from the British Library

Print ISBN: 978 1 4728 0950 6

PDF ebook ISBN: 978 1 4728 0951 3

ePub ebook ISBN: 978 1 4728 0952 0

Index by Mark Swift

Typeset in Sabon and Myriad Pro

Originated by PDQ Media, Bungay, UK

Printed in China through Worldprint Ltd

15 16 17 18 19 10 9 8 7 6 5 4 3 2 1

Osprey Publishing supports the Woodland Trust, the UK's leading woodland conservation charity. Between 2014 and 2018 our donations are being spent on their Centenary Woods project in the UK.

www.ospreypublishing.com

ACKNOWLEDGMENTS

The author wishes to thank German maritime experts Dorothee Jensen and Simon Jenson for assisting him with his research in Hamburg and northern Germany.

PHOTOGRAPHS

Unless otherwise noted, photos are from the collection of the author.

CONTENTS

GERMAN COMMERCE RAIDERS 1914–18

INTRODUCTION

In the first two decades of its existence the German Kaiserliche Marine (Imperial Navy) gave little consideration to the strategy of *Kreuzerkrieg*, or raiding enemy commerce. During this period the Kaiserliche Marine was commanded by two army generals (Albrecht von Stosch and Georg Leo von Caprivi) who believed that the primary task of the Navy was coastal defense, and furthermore, Kaiser Wilhelm I showed little interest in naval expansion. Beginning in the mid-1880s colonial duties were added to the responsibilities of the Kaiserliche Marine as Germany established colonies in Africa and Asia. New construction began on several classes of protected and unprotected cruisers termed *Auslandskreuzer* (overseas cruisers), designed for duties in foreign waters. Thus the navy was a mixed collection of coastal defense vessels, torpedo boats, and overseas cruisers modeled on the theories of the *Jeune École*, when Kaiser Wilhelm II came to power in June 1888. Wilhelm II, unlike his grandfather, took a keen interest in naval affairs and pushed for an expansion of the Kaiserliche Marine. He believed that increasing German influence in world affairs (*Weltmacht*) could only be continued through naval expansion (*Seemacht*) and increased maritime trade. Wilhelm II was impressed with the large battle-fleet theories espoused by Alfred Thayer Mahan, but was equally interested in demonstrating Germany's global presence through cruiser squadrons stationed overseas in its new colonial possessions. Furthermore the rapid growth of the German merchant marine and the expansion of maritime trade around the world demanded an increased naval presence in foreign waters. With France and Russia seen as Germany's foremost enemies in the early 1890s, the head of the Reichsmarineamt (Imperial Naval Office), Admiral Friedrich von Hollmann, embarked on a balanced construction program building the first ocean-going battleships for the Kaiserliche Marine as well as new Auslandskreuzer designed to conduct commerce raiding operations.

Kaiser Wilhelm II speaking with Admiral Friedrich von Hollmann. An advocate of commerce raiding, Hollmann instituted the Kaiserliche Marine's Hilfskreuzer program. (Bundesarchiv, Bild 134-B2779, photo: o.Ang)

During the 1890s Hollmann also examined the potential usefulness of auxiliary commerce raiders in a naval war. Only 30 years before, a handful of Confederate merchant vessels, converted into auxiliary cruisers, had crippled Union seaborne trade through a combination of sunken tonnage and highly inflated insurance rates during the American Civil War. Hollmann pondered whether the growing number of fast ocean liners of Germany's major shipping lines could be similarly converted and deployed in wartime. In the 1890s, new ocean liners tended to be capable of speeds greater than or equal to those of most large warships and several navies examined the possibility of their conversion to auxiliary cruisers. Beginning in 1885 the Deutsche Reichspost (Imperial Postal Service) issued lucrative subsidies to German shipping lines for delivery of mail throughout the world as a way of fostering the growth of the German merchant marine. Lines that partook of these subsidies were required in wartime, however, to turn control of their vessels over to the Kaiserliche Marine for potential military service. Almost all German shipping lines were part of this arrangement, most importantly the two largest, Hamburg Amerika and Norddeutscher Lloyd. In 1888 Hamburg Amerika launched the first of four fast German liners, *Auguste Victoria*, *Columbia*, *Normannia*, and *Fürst Bismarck*, which were built with reinforced decks that could support the mounting of naval guns in time of war. Subsequent fast German liners were similarly equipped, as per the terms mandated by their Reichspost subsidy contracts. In 1895 *Normannia* was briefly requisitioned by the Navy and armed in order to examine the potential of the liner in the role of auxiliary warship; the results of the exercises were positive and she became the first *Hilfskreuzer* (auxiliary cruiser) of the Kaiserliche Marine. As a result Hollmann and Wilhelm II pushed for the formal creation of a reserve fleet of auxiliary cruisers drawn from the liners of the major shipping lines; from that point on the commanders of all liners earmarked for conversion into Hilfskreuzer carried concealed mobilization orders to be opened in the event of war.

German pursuit of Weltmacht eventually fumbled its way into an unforeseen naval rivalry with Great Britain, beginning in the late 1890s. German support of Russia's annexation of Port Arthur and the Liaodong Peninsula in 1895, Germany's occupation of Tsingtau in China in November 1897 as a permanent Far Eastern naval base, and Wilhelm II's tacit support for German arms sales to the Boer republics in the Second Boer War created a wave of anti-German sentiment in Great Britain. Realizing that the Kaiserliche Marine did not have the strength to uphold Germany's growing world influence in the face of British opposition, the Kaiser came to the conclusion that Great Britain and the Royal Navy were now the primary obstacles denying Germany her place in the sun.

This sudden shift in diplomatic direction brought a dramatic change in naval leadership and strategy, embodied in Admiral Alfred von Tirpitz, who was appointed head of the Reichsmarineamt in 1897. Tirpitz was also a follower of Mahan's theories of sea power and fostered the belief that the Royal Navy

Normannia, the Kaiserliche Marine's first Hilfskreuzer.

was the primary threat to Germany's overseas ambitions. He created his own variant of Mahan's ideas of fleet concentration: the *Risikogedanke*, or risk theory, in which Germany would maintain a large enough fleet that if the British attempted to engage it, the result would be an *Entscheidungsschlacht*, or decisive battle, which would cripple the Royal Navy to such an extent that it would be unable to maintain an effective blockade on German ports or withstand a challenge from another naval power. In other words, Tirpitz gambled that Britain would be deterred from fighting a war with Germany which might result in the Royal Navy being crippled or defeated in what would essentially be a "Mexican standoff". It was a high-risk and rigid strategy based on aggressive brinksmanship and the status quo of diplomatic alliances at the end of the 19th century; furthermore it dictated that all German warship construction had to be dedicated to units, primarily battleships, destined for the High Seas Fleet stationed in home waters. Although the survival of British industry and society itself depended upon a constant flow of seaborne imports from across the globe, attacking British maritime commerce was ironically a secondary consideration for Tirpitz. A sustained campaign against British commerce was only to be implemented in the event of a German defeat in a decisive battle with the Royal Navy in the North Sea; furthermore the Risikogedanke strategy presupposed that a war with Britain would not last long enough for a British blockade of German ports to have any serious effect on the course of the conflict.

Although Tirpitz's strategic vision was almost exclusively fixated on the North Sea Theater, he coupled a limited Kreuzerkrieg offensive to his wartime strategy. As a small number of navy vessels were stationed abroad in Germany's colonies and new ocean liners were being built according to Hollmann's earlier Hilfskreuzer specifications, Tirpitz believed an attack on British commerce with these vessels could draw British units away from the North Sea theater, thus improving the odds of victory for the High Seas Fleet in the anticipated Entscheidungsschlacht. The Ostasiatische Kreuzergeschwader (East Asian Cruiser Squadron, simply referred to as the Kreuzergeschwader) was the Kaiserliche Marine's only dedicated overseas squadron, having been permanently formed in 1894 at the beginning of the First Sino-Japanese War. Operating from its base at Tsingtau (established by the Kaiserliche Marine in 1897) on the Shantung Peninsula, the Kreuzergeschwader was responsible for representing German interests and showing the flag in the Orient and Pacific. Due primarily to pressure from the Kaiser, German shipping lines, the Reichskolonialamt (Imperial Colonial Office), and other colonial interests, Tirpitz was compelled to maintain a reasonably strong force of several armored cruisers and light cruisers for overseas service. The few armored cruisers constructed for the Kaiserliche Marine were designed to be dual-purpose overseas station ships and powerful scouts for the battle fleet; the rigid terms of the Risikogedanke allowed for no purpose-built overseas vessels. Likewise light

Armored cruiser *Gneisenau* taking on coal at Tsingtau in 1911. The primary motivation for Germany's acquisition of colonies in the Pacific in the late 19th century was the establishment of coaling stations, thus allowing for a worldwide naval presence.

cruisers built from 1897 to 1912 (the 33 units of the Gazelle, Bremen, Königsberg, Dresden, Kolberg, Magdeburg, and Karlsruhe classes of light cruisers) were designed for use with the battle fleet as well as overseas duties. In the first decade of the 20th century German naval strategists concluded that, given the remote location of Tsingtau, in time of war the ships of the Kreuzergeschwader were to be ordered to proceed to sea and conduct cruiser warfare against the enemy's shipping lanes.

A handful of other warships operating outside of German home waters in 1914 had similar commerce raiding instructions to the Kreuzergeschwader. By 1914 Germany's global commitments had compelled the Kaiserliche Marine to create several overseas stations: the Mittelmeer Station (Mediterranean), Ostamerikanische Station (western Atlantic and Caribbean), Westamerikanische Station (eastern Pacific), Australische Station (southern Pacific and Australia), Ostafrikanische Station (East Africa), and Westafrikanische Station (West Africa). Each station was patrolled by a cruiser or a handful of ocean-going gunboats. Cruisers were never permanently on station and they were rotated home for maintenance overhauls as, with the exception of Tsingtau, there were no naval bases overseas with extensive repair facilities. Ships operating on the Australische, Ostafrikanische, and Westafrikanische stations had the ability to coal and undertake minor repairs in German colonial ports in the Pacific and Africa. Ships on the Mittelmeer Station had to rely on the ports of allied nations (Austria-Hungary and Italy) while those on the Ostamerikanische Station operated out of the island of St Thomas in the Caribbean through an agreement with a friendly Denmark. The nearest friendly base for ships on the Westamerikanische Station was Tsingtau, however. In time of peace when coaling in a German port was impracticable, warships stationed abroad were given funds to purchase coal in foreign ports, primarily in the United States and South America.

In time of war, German warships would be unable to sufficiently coal in neutral ports as neutrality laws prevented belligerent warships from staying more than 24 hours in a neutral port and they could only take on a minimum of coal (typically just enough to get a warship to the nearest friendly port). As German colonial ports were widely spread and, particularly in a war with Great Britain, as the odds were high that these ports would be blockaded and/or captured, the Kaiserliche Marine developed an ingenious worldwide network for resupplying its warships operating abroad. The *Etappendienst* was a force of colliers and merchant vessels (most belonging to German shipping lines although a few were from likely-neutral nations), based in ports of likely-neutral nations, chartered by the Kaiserliche Marine to supply its cruisers at sea in time of war. The world was divided into fifteen *Etappen* (zones), headed by naval officers who were responsible for the purchase of coal and supplies and for dispatching the *Etappenschiffe* (*Etappen* ships) to rendezvous points with warships at sea. While neutral nations had to follow strict protocols regarding the supplying of belligerent warships in their ports, there were few regulations regarding the activities of

Valparaiso Harbor, Chile. Neutral ports like this were the lairs of the Etappenschiffe where coal and provisions could be purchased for raiders. Officers of the Etappendienst also relayed enemy shipping information via wireless transmitters aboard German ships, providing valuable intelligence. (Library of Congress LC-DIG-npcc-19938)

A typical Etappenschiff was the 3,776-ton freighter *Corrientes* of the Hamburg-Südamerikanischen Dampfschiffahrtsgesellschaft. She was part of Etappe Brasilien and supplied the cruiser *Dresden* in August 1914.

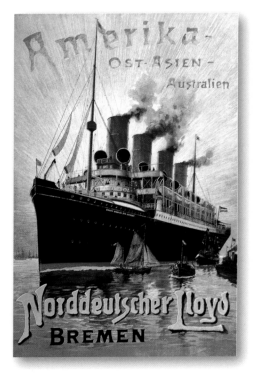

In return for Deutsche Reichspost mail subsidies, several German shipping lines agreed to turn control of their fastest liners, such as the *Kaiser Wilhelm der Grosse* of the Norddeutscher Lloyd shown here, over to the Kaiserliche Marine in wartime for conversion into Hilfskreuzer.

belligerent merchant vessels, and the Kaiserliche Marine believed that friendly neutral nations would overlook the indirect supply of its warships as long as it was through merchant vessels. There was no shortage of potential Etappenschiffe thanks to the militarization terms of the Reichspost subsidies. Merchantmen designated as potential Etappenschiffe carried sealed orders which their captains were to follow in the event of war.

As the Etappendienst would also be used to support the commerce raiding operations of the Hilfskreuzer, Tirpitz came to look favorably on the Hilfskreuzer program, as auxiliary cruisers raiding British commerce around the world in concert with warships stationed abroad were likely to draw warships away from the main British battle fleet in the North Sea without diminishing the strength of the High Seas Fleet. Great Britain followed German precedent and up to 1914 a second, subtle naval arms race began between the two nations – to match the threat of each other's armed ocean liners in time of war. Few in the public knew that the great liners of the major British and German shipping lines vying for the Blue Riband Atlantic speed record were built with potential naval service in mind. In 1913, however, most modern warships had greatly improved speeds over their 19th-century counterparts and the Kaiserliche Marine instituted a new set of technical requirements for its Hilfskreuzer. Liners brought into Hilfskreuzer service had to be able to maintain a minimum speed of 18 knots, possess a cruising range of over 10,000 miles at 10 knots, have reinforced mounts on their decks for 10.5cm and 15cm cannon, possess coal bunkers that protected machinery and munitions storage rooms below the waterline, have a double hull, and be equipped with up-to-date wireless communications equipment. In 1914 only 13 liners under the German flag met these requirements (ironically the Royal Navy believed that the Kaiserliche Marine had over 40 liners earmarked for conversion into Hilfskreuzer in 1914). Hilfskreuzer liners in home waters at the beginning of a conflict would be armed in navy yards; those caught abroad would meet German warships at prearranged rendezvous points where they would be armed at sea.

To coordinate the activities of the Kreuzergeschwader, overseas cruisers, Hilfskreuzer, and Etappendienst, the Kaiserliche Marine turned to the relatively new technology of wireless communication. In the 19th century, Great Britain laid a massive network of submarine telegraph cables across the globe for military and civilian use and held a near monopoly in transoceanic communications; Germany in contrast had only one submarine cable to the United States via France, Spain, and the Azores. At the time other nations, including Germany, used British cables to send civilian and military messages around the globe. Realizing that in time of war these avenues of communication would be cut off, the German government heavily subsidized the creation of a worldwide wireless network beginning in the early 20th century. Wireless communication also offered an easier and less-expensive alternative to submarine cables and the German firm of Telefunken quickly became the world's premier manufacturer of wireless equipment. In 1909 a wireless transmitter was constructed at Nauen, just west of Berlin, which could send messages up to 5,000 kilometers, to be then relayed to other

The wireless station at Nauen outside of Berlin, which had a broadcast range of 5,000km.

stations throughout Germany's colonies. Stations with powerful transmitters, with ranges of 1,800–3,000 kilometers, were set up at Kamina in Togoland, Windhuk in German Southwest Africa, Tsingtau in China, Yap in the Caroline Islands, and Nauru in the Marshall Islands. There were smaller transmitters located in German East Africa and the South Pacific as well. While Germany's ambitious worldwide wireless network was not yet complete by the outbreak of World War I, most of the seas that contained the world's major shipping lanes were under the German wireless umbrella.

GERMAN NAVAL UNITS ABROAD IN AUGUST 1914

On August 4, 1914, the *Admiralstab* (Imperial Admiralty Staff) in Berlin relayed the British declaration of war on Germany to German warships and vessels abroad, beginning the Kreuzerkrieg against Allied commerce. Via the Nauen transmitter, merchant captains and Etappendienst officers were instructed to open their wartime orders. The Kreuzergeschwader numbered five warships in August 1914: the armored cruisers *Scharnhorst* and *Gneisenau*, and the light cruisers *Emden*, *Leipzig*, and *Nürnberg*. Vizeadmiral Maximilian Reichsgraf von Spee, commander of the Kreuzergeschwader, was conducting a summer training cruise with *Scharnhorst* and *Gneisenau* through Germany's Pacific colonies when Archduke Franz Ferdinand was assassinated. He was at the island of Ponape on August 4 and two days later was joined there by *Nürnberg*, which had been on her way back to Tsingtau after a tour of duty on the Westamerikanische Station. *Leipzig* was off the coast of Mexico, having just relieved *Nürnberg*, and *Emden* was moored in Tsingtau.

Spee received orders to keep as much of the Kreuzergeschwader together as possible, and operate as a small fleet-in-being which would threaten Allied sea lanes and tie down as many Allied warships as possible[1]. Other Kaiserliche Marine warships abroad on August 4 included the light cruisers *Dresden* and *Karlsruhe* in the Caribbean and the light cruiser *Königsberg* in German East Africa. To support the operations of warships abroad and the Hilfskreuzer, the Etappendienst mobilized 122 support vessels totaling 554,558 tons, stationed in ports around the world: Etappe Batavia – 8 ships (38,423 tons); Etappe Brasilien – 12 ships (55,637 tons); Etappe China – 2 ships (7,506 tons); Etappe Japan – 4 ships (24,156 tons); Etappe La Plata – 9 ships (48,486 tons); Etappe Manila – 12 ships (44,691 tons); Etappe Mittelmeer – 6 ships (30,864 tons); Etappe Nordamerika – 21 ships (91,585 tons); Etappe Ostafrika – 3 ships (11,050 tons); Etappe Peru – 2 ships (12,977 tons); Etappe San Francisco – 3 ships (9,373 tons); Etappe Tsingtau – 12 ships (43,861 tons); Etappe Valparaiso – 10 ships (64,529 tons); Etappe Westafrika – 12 ships (47,714 tons); Etappe Westindien – 6 ships (23,706 tons).

By 1914 the Kaiserliche Marine had 11 liners earmarked for conversion into Hilfskreuzer in time of war. Their conversions were prioritized into two tiers: the frontline vessels to be converted immediately were *Viktoria Luise* (ex-*Deutschland*) of Hamburg Amerika and *Kaiser Wilhelm II*, *Kronprinz Wilhelm*, and *Kaiser Wilhelm der Grosse* of Norddeutscher Lloyd; a reserve tier of liners to be converted after the frontline vessels had been equipped (or to replace them if they were not immediately available) and included *Cap Finisterre* and *Cap Trafalgar* of Hamburg-Südamerikanischen Dampfschiffahrtsgesellschaft and *Kronprinzessin Cecilie*, *Prinz Ludwig*, *Prinz Eitel Friedrich*, *George Washington*, and *Prinz Friedrich Wilhelm* of Norddeutscher Lloyd. On August 4 only two of the frontline Hilfskreuzer were able to be commissioned: *Kaiser Wilhelm der Grosse* was in Bremerhaven and *Kronprinz Wilhelm* sailed from New York on August 5 before British cruisers could establish a patrol off the coast. *Viktoria Luise*, moored in Hamburg, was armed but was quickly decommissioned when it was discovered her worn engines could not raise enough speed to effectively serve as a Hilfskreuzer. *Kaiser Wilhelm II* was westbound across the Atlantic on August 4 and evaded British patrols to slip into New York on August 6; she was bottled up there by British patrols afterwards. Of the reserve Hilfskreuzer, only two were commissioned: *Prinz Eitel Friedrich* was in Tsingtau and *Cap Trafalgar* was in Buenos Aires but was able to sail out of the Rio de la Plata on August 23. *Cap Finisterre* and *Prinz Ludwig* were both in Germany but their engines could not produce enough speed to meet the Hilfskreuzer requirements. *George Washington* was caught in New York and unable to leave. *Kronprinzessin Cecilie* was eastward-bound out of New York when war threatened and she turned around, putting into Bar Harbor, Maine, on the evening of August 4 to avoid British patrols. Finally, *Prinz Friedrich Wilhelm* was in the middle of a North Sea cruise on August 4 and put into Odda, Norway, to avoid potential capture.

Color photo of the former German liners *George Washington*, *Amerika*, *Kronprinzessin Cecilie*, and *Kaiser Wilhelm II* anchored in the Patuxent River in Maryland on the eve of World War II. Three of these vessels were designated as Hilfskreuzer but were unable to leave American ports after the war began. They were eventually confiscated by the American government in April 1917 and served as the American transports USS *George Washington*, USS *America*, USS *Mount Vernon*, and USS *Agamemnon* respectively. *George Washington* and *America* also served as troopships in World War II.

1   As *Scharnhorst*, *Gneisenau*, and *Nürnberg* did not directly take part in commerce raiding, their wartime careers are not covered in this narrative; see Osprey's CAM 248, *Coronel and Falklands 1914*.

Thus when the Kaiserliche Marine began its surface campaign against British commerce, it deployed four light cruisers and four Hilfskreuzer. The following three chapters provide the technical details and brief career summaries of these vessels (as well as two spontaneous Hilfskreuzer conversions).

THE CRUISERS

SMS *Dresden*

Dimensions:	length: 386ft 10in
	beam: 44ft 4in
	draft: 18ft
Displacement:	3,664 tons
Complement:	361
Armament:	ten 10.5cm Krupp SK L/40 guns, two located side-by-side fore, six amidships (three on each side), and two side-by-side aft; two 450mm torpedo tubes, underwater, one on each broadside
Machinery:	four Parsons turbines, coal-fired by 12 marine boilers, generating up to 15,000 IHP and turning two screws at a maximum speed of 24 knots
Maximum Range:	3,600 nautical miles at 14 knots
Protection:	conning tower: 3.9in sides, ¾in roof
	armored deck: 3.1in amidships tapering to ¾in on both ends with 1.8in of sloped armor on the sides
	gun shields: 2in
Coal Capacity:	790 tons
Builder:	Blohm & Voss of Hamburg (1908)

Dresden was off Saint Thomas in the Virgin Islands on July 31, 1914, on her way back to Germany having been on a tour of duty in the Caribbean since December 1913, when she received a wireless message to stay on station in the Caribbean due to the political tension in Europe. Assuming that he would be instructed to commence commerce raiding if war was declared, *Dresden*'s skipper, Fregattenkapitän Fritz Emil Lüdecke, headed for the sea lanes off northeastern Brazil. After the war began, Lüdecke stopped four empty British merchantmen on August 6–8 but let them all go after disabling their wireless equipment; Lüdecke seemed to lack the resolve of other German raider commanders who had no qualms about sinking empty enemy vessels. On August 15 *Dresden* took her first prize, the 3,352-ton British freighter *Hyades*. Lüdecke then sailed for small Ilha da Trindade, 500 miles off the coast of central Brazil, to meet a collier from Etappe La Plata. After several days of coaling and maintenance on her turbines *Dresden* headed south and captured and sank the 4,223-ton British freighter *Holmwood* on August 26. Lüdecke continued south and received word from the Admiralstab instructing *Dresden* to raid in concert with *Leipzig* in the Pacific. After a lengthy period of coaling and engine repairs off the southern tip of South America, *Dresden* rounded Cape Horn and headed for the Pacific. On October 3 Lüdecke received a wireless message ordering him to immediately meet Vizeadmiral Graf Spee and the Kreuzergeschwader at Easter Island. The rendezvous was made on October 12 and

A 10.5cm gun turret lying amid the debris of *Dresden*'s wreck off Más á Tierra. (Courtesy of Daniel Malfanti, Instructor de Buceo Deportivo y Técnico IANTD)

Bow view of SMS *Dresden*.

from there *Dresden* participated in the battle of Coronel as part of the Kreuzergeschwader. *Dresden* managed to drive off the armed merchant cruiser HMS *Otranto* after a few shots and briefly engaged the light cruiser HMS *Glasgow* with *Leipzig*.

Dresden played even less of a part in the battle of the Falkland Islands. Spee ordered his light cruisers to break off and scatter when the British battlecruisers and cruisers began their pursuit, while *Scharnhorst* and *Gneisenau* attempted to cover their retreat. *Dresden* was furthest away from the pursuing British and her engineers were able to bring her turbines to deliver 27 knots. While the British concentrated their fire on *Leipzig* and *Nürnberg*, *Dresden* pulled ahead and disappeared to the southwest in a squall, successfully escaping into the waterways west of Tierra del Fuego. The Germans had the advantage of modern charts and Lüdecke was able to avoid British patrols and receive supplies from Etappenschiffe; most British maps of the area dated back to the voyages of Charles Darwin. After lingering around the Cockburn and Barbara Channels for nearly two months, Lüdecke decided to head for the Pacific, intent on resuming raiding. *Dresden* set sail on February 14, 1915, with the Etappenschiff *Sierra Cordoba* scouting 100 miles ahead. After a fruitless cruise northward for two weeks *Dresden* finally took a prize, the 1,694-ton British bark *Conway Castle*, on February 27. Without any sightings of *Dresden* for over three months, the British finally calculated the location of the phantom cruiser in early March through intercepted and deciphered messages from an Etappenschiff. On March 14, as Lüdecke awaited the arrival of an Etappenschiff (the one the British were tracking) off the island of Más á Tierra, just over 400 miles off the west coast of Chile, he was ambushed by the armored cruiser HMS *Kent*, light cruiser *Glasgow*, and auxiliary cruiser *Orama*. After a brief gun battle, *Dresden* was scuttled and her surviving crew were interned in Chile.

SMS *Emden*

(Same technical details as *Dresden* (sister ships of the same class) except for machinery, maximum range, and builder.)

Dimensions:	length: 386ft 10in
	beam: 44ft 4in
	draft: 18ft
Displacement:	3,664 tons
Complement:	361
Armament:	ten 10.5cm Krupp SK L/40 guns, two located side-by-side fore, six amidships (three on each side), and two side-by-side aft; two 450mm torpedo tubes, underwater, one on each broadside
Machinery:	two vertical triple expansion engines, coal-fired by 12 marine boilers, generating up to 13,500 IHP and turning two screws at a maximum speed of 23.5 knots
Maximum Range:	3,760 nautical miles at 12 knots
Protection:	conning tower: 3.9in sides, ¾in roof
	armored deck: 3.1in amidships tapering to ¾in on both ends with 1.8in of sloped armor on the sides
	gun shields: 2in
Coal Capacity:	790 tons
Builder:	Kaiserliche Werft of Danzig (1909)

On August 6, 1914, *Emden*, under the command of Korvettenkapitän Karl von Müller, sailed from Tsingtau and rendezvoused with the Kreuzergeschwader in the Marianas Islands several days later. Müller persuaded Spee that a cruiser should be detached to independently raid Allied shipping in the Indian Ocean and the admiral gave the mission to Müller as *Emden* was the fastest cruiser in the Kreuzergeschwader. On August 14, *Emden* headed west, accompanied by the collier *Markomannia*. For the next several weeks *Emden* cruised south-by-west through the Dutch East Indies expecting to meet with supply ships from Etappe Batavia but none were at their rendezvous points. On August 27 *Emden* was approached by the Dutch coastal defense ship *Tromp* south of Celebes and Müller learned from the *Tromp*'s commander the reason why none of the Etappenschiffe had appeared; the usually sympathetic Dutch government had insisted upon strict neutrality protocols in the East Indies, fearful of Japanese aggression in the archipelago if the Dutch showed any favoritism to German ships. Frustrated, Müller sailed westward along the southern and western coasts of Java and Sumatra and then headed northward towards the Bay of Bengal. On the evening of September 9 *Emden*'s luck changed when she stopped the Greek collier *Pontoporos* carrying 6,500 tons of good coal owned by the British. The *Pontoporos*'s skipper agreed to charter his vessel to the Kaiserliche Marine for a fee when asked by Müller, and *Emden* now had all the coal she needed for some time. For the next several days *Emden* cruised the Bay of Bengal, taking seven British prizes: September 10 – 3,413-ton freighter *Indus*; September 11 – 6,102-ton freighter *Lovat*; September 12 – 4,657-ton freighter *Kabinga* (released to remove prisoners) and 3,544-ton freighter *Killin*; September 13 – 7,615-ton freighter *Diplomat*; September 14 – 4,028-ton freighter *Trabboch*; September 15 – 4,775-ton freighter *Clan Matheson*. *Emden* was aided in raiding by a retractable dummy fourth funnel constructed by her crew which made her appear like a British cruiser from a distance.

On September 18 *Emden* coaled and set a course due west for the port of Madras. With the dummy funnel raised, Müller brazenly took his ship into brightly lit Madras harbor on the evening of September 22, turned his spotlights on, and opened fire.

Emden sailing out of Penang harbor after sinking the Russian 3,530-ton protected cruiser *Zhemchug* on the morning of October 22, 1914.

Members of *Emden*'s landing party on Direction Island preparing to take supplies out to the commandeered schooner *Ayesha*. The 47-man landing party, commanded by Kapitänleutnant Hellmuth von Mücke, witnessed *Emden*'s final battle but escaped across the Indian Ocean. After traveling up the Arabian Peninsula and warding off Bedouin attacks, Mücke and his surviving men arrived in Constantinople in late May 1915 and from there returned to Germany.

A group of Australians posing in front of the wreck of *Emden* on North Keeling Island.

The damage inflicted by *Emden*'s bombardment was minimal but several oil storage tanks were destroyed; the worst damage caused was to British morale as the German cruiser was able to raid a large British port and escape without a scratch. The Allies intensified their efforts to track down *Emden* but as Müller maintained radio silence they could only rely on chance visual sightings. *Emden* made a clean getaway however and took six additional British prizes off Ceylon over the next few days: September 25 – 3,650-ton freighter *King Lud*; September 26 – 3,314-ton freighter *Tymeric*, 4,437-ton freighter *Gryfevale* (released to remove prisoners), and 4,337-ton collier *Buresk* (prize crew put aboard and retained as a collier); September 27 – 3,500-ton freighter *Ribera* and 4,147-ton freighter *Foyle*. Müller then sailed southward for several days and anchored off Diego Garcia on October 9–10 to conduct routine maintenance on the engines and boilers and to clean the hull.

Emden then sailed northward along the western coast of the Maldive Islands and soon took another succession of British prizes: October 16 – 3,948-ton freighter *Clan Grant*, 473-ton dredger *Ponrabel*, and 4,806-ton freighter *Benmohr*; October 18 – 7,562-ton freighter *Trolius*, 5,596-ton freighter *St. Egbert* (released to remove prisoners), and 4,542-ton collier

A **EMDEN**

Emden is certainly the most documented of Germany's cruiser-raiders of World War I, her daring exploits and the gentlemanly character of her skipper and crew making fascinating reading material. Added to this was her swath of destruction, sinking 78,742 tons of Allied shipping over a two-month period, making her the scourge of her enemies who at one point had 16 warships hunting this solitary raider, thus achieving exactly the kind of objective the Admiralstab hoped for from commerce raiding. *Emden*'s most daring and brazen engagements came toward the end of her brief raiding career. As *Emden* cruised eastward across the Indian Ocean after raiding the waters off Ceylon and the Maldives in October 1914, Korvettenkapitän Müller learned from passing neutral vessels that light Allied warships were operating out of the port of Penang in Malaysia and he decided to attempt to ambush one or several of them with a surprise attack. Early on the morning of October 22 *Emden*, disguised with its dummy funnel and flying a British ensign, sailed into Penang harbor and spotted the Russian 3,530-ton protected cruiser *Zhemchug* at anchor; *Emden* sent her to the bottom with a combination of two torpedoes and gunfire. As *Emden* was heading towards the sea the 310-ton French destroyer *Mousquet* entered the harbor and after a short exchange of gunfire *Mousquet* was turned into a burning wreck.

After making a clean getaway, Müller headed south in order to coal and then attack the wireless and cable stations on Direction Island in the Cocos group south of Sumatra. On the morning of November 9 *Emden* arrived off Direction Island and sent a landing party ashore to destroy the wireless and cable stations, but not before their staff sent out an SOS identifying the German cruiser. An hour after the wireless mast was knocked down an Australian light cruiser, the 6,000-ton HMAS *Sydney*, appeared on the horizon and Müller, leaving his landing party ashore, steamed seaward to meet the intruder. Unfortunately for *Emden*, *Sydney* was armed with eight 6in guns and was 4 knots faster. The battle began at 0940hrs and *Emden* managed to strike *Sydney* a few times but eventually the heavier armament of the latter battered the more lightly armed German cruiser; *Emden*'s 10.5cm guns lacked the punch to cause significant damage to her opponent. Finally with all of *Emden*'s guns knocked out and over half of her crew dead or wounded, Müller ran his crippled ship ashore on North Keeling Island at 11:15 in order to save his surviving men.

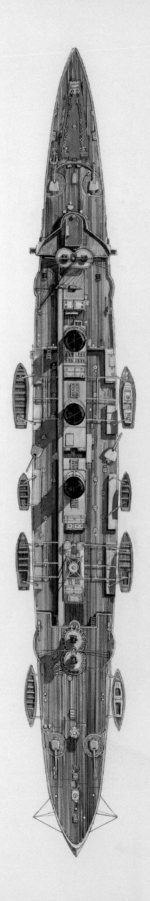

Exford (prize crew put aboard and retained as a collier); October 19 – 5,146-ton freighter *Chilkana*. Having caused considerable chaos off Ceylon and the Maldives, Müller decided to change his area of operations and headed east across the Indian Ocean. *Emden* raided Penang harbor, sinking two Allied warships on October 22 and then headed south, taking one last prize (October 30 – 3,554-ton British freighter *Newburn* – released to remove prisoners) before being sunk in a gunnery duel with the Australian light cruiser HMAS *Sydney* off the Cocos Islands on November 9 (for the details of *Emden*'s raid on Penang and her battle with *Sydney* see Plate A).

SMS *Karlsruhe*

Dimensions:	length: 466ft 6in
	beam: 44ft 11in
	draft: 18ft
Displacement:	4,900 tons
Complement:	373
Armament:	twelve 10.5cm Krupp SK L/45 guns, two located side-by-side fore, eight amidships (four on each side), and two side-by-side aft; two 500mm torpedo tubes, underwater, one on each broadside; up to 120 mines
Machinery:	two marine turbines, coal- and oil-fired by 14 marine boilers (ten coal-fired, four oil-fired), generating up to 26,000 IHP and turning two screws up to 27 knots
Maximum Range:	5,500 nautical miles at 12 knots
Protection:	armored belt: 2¼in amidships tapering to ¾in at the bow with no stern protection
	conning tower: 4in on the sides, ¾in on the roof
	armored deck: 2¼in forward tapering to 1½in amidships to ¾in at the stern with 1½in sloped armor connecting the deck with the belt
	gun shields: 2in
Coal Capacity:	1,300 tons (200 tons of oil)
Builder:	Germaniaweft of Kiel (1914)

Karlsruhe was sent to the Ostamerikanische Station in July to relieve *Dresden* and was sailing among the remote islands of the Bahamas to avoid being caught in a port in the event of war when hostilities commenced. *Karlsruhe*'s commander, Fregattenkapitän Erich Köhler, received orders to attack Allied commerce off North America; he also had standing orders to rendezvous with the Hilfskreuzer *Kronprinz Wilhelm* and arm her, according to prewar instructions. On August 6 *Karlsruhe* met *Kronprinz Wilhelm* 120 miles north of Watling Island in the Bahamas and transferred guns and ammunition to the liner. The meeting was interrupted by the sudden appearance to the south of the British armored cruiser *Suffolk*. *Karlsruhe* and *Kronprinz Wilhelm* immediately steamed off. *Suffolk*, later joined by the light cruiser *Bristol*, chased *Karlsruhe* but Köhler eventually lost his pursuers later that evening under the cover of darkness.

Köhler calculated that there was too much enemy activity in the Caribbean for successful operations and decided to head southward for the sea lanes off Brazil. Along the way *Karlsruhe* took her first three British prizes: August 18 – 4,650-ton freighter *Bowes Castle*; August 31 – 4,336-ton collier *Strathroy* (prize crew put aboard and retained as a collier); September 3 – 4,338-ton freighter *Maple Branch*. Köhler then headed for the sea lanes off the northern Brazilian coast, this time with the Etappenschiffe *Crefeld* and *Rio Negro* sailing 20 miles out on each side of *Karlsruhe*, serving as scouts for the

SMS *Karlsruhe*, steaming at high speed. (Bundesarchiv, Bild 134-C0152, photo: o.Ang)

cruiser. For the next six weeks *Karlsruhe* cruised back and forth on a northeasterly course and captured an additional 12 merchantmen (all British unless otherwise noted): September 14 – 5,159-ton freighter *Highland Hope*; September 17 – 5,706 collier *Indrani* (prize crew put aboard and retained as a collier); September 21 – 3,804-ton Dutch steamer *Maria* (carrying a British cargo of wheat) and 3,816-ton freighter *Cornish City*; September 22 – 3,817-ton collier *Rio Iguassu*; October 5 – 5,810-ton collier *Farn* (prize crew put aboard and retained as a collier); October 6 – 5,018-ton freighter *Niceto de Larrinaga*; October 7 – 3,384-ton freighter *Lynrowan*; October 8 – 4,635-ton freighter *Cervantes* and 4,408-ton freighter *Pruth*; October 18 – 3,021-ton freighter *Glanton*; October 23 – 2,752-ton freighter *Hurtsdale*.

By October 25 Köhler learned from increased enemy wireless traffic that the British were closing in on his area of operations; he had anticipated this as he had to release the Etappenschiff *Crefeld* with a full load of prisoners, which arrived in the Canary Islands on October 22. Assuming that the British would begin searching the northern Brazilian coast, Köhler, on October 25, decided to head for the Caribbean, which he believed would be relatively undefended as the British were now preoccupied in his former hunting grounds and by the approach of the Kreuzergeschwader in the Pacific. On October 26, *Karlsruhe* captured her last and largest prize: the 10,328-ton British liner *Vandyck*, scuttled after the crew and passengers were brought aboard the Etappenschiff *Asuncion*. As *Karlsruhe* made her way northwards into the Caribbean with her remaining auxiliaries, a massive explosion erupted aboard the cruiser on the evening of November 4, blowing away the bow, bridge, and everything ahead of the forward funnel including Köhler and 262 of his crew. Before what was left of the cruiser sank, 123 survivors of the explosion were able to abandon ship; the cause of the explosion remains a mystery to this day. The *Karlsruhe*'s surviving First Officer, Kapitänleutnant Studt, brought the surviving crew and all of the prisoners from *Karlsruhe*'s auxiliaries aboard the Etappenschiff *Rio Negro*, intent on keeping news of the sinking of the cruiser from the Allies for as long as possible. Studt took *Rio Negro* across the Atlantic and through the British blockade, finally reaching Hamburg in mid-December 1914. The British continued to search for *Karlsruhe* until wreckage from the cruiser washed ashore on the Caribbean island of St Vincent in March 1915.

SMS *Königsberg*

Dimensions:	length: 376ft 8in
	beam: 43ft 4in
	draft: 17ft
Displacement:	3,390 tons
Complement:	322
Armament:	ten 10.5cm Krupp SK L/40 guns, two located side-by-side fore, six amidships (three on each side), and two side-by-side aft; ten 37mm QF guns; two 450mm torpedo tubes, underwater, one on each broadside
Machinery:	two vertical triple expansion engines, coal-fired by 11 marine boilers, generating up to 12,000 IHP and turning two screws at a maximum speed of 23 knots
Maximum Range:	5,750 nautical miles at 12 knots
Protection:	conning tower: 3.9in on the sides, ¾in on the roof
	armored deck: 3.1in amidships tapering to ¾in on both ends with 1.8in of sloped armor on the sides
	gun shields: 2in
Coal Capacity:	820 tons
Builder:	Kaiserliche Werft of Kiel (1907)

The onset of war in Europe found *Königsberg* in Dar es Salaam in German East Africa, serving as the station ship for the Ostafrikanische Station since her arrival from Kiel on June 6, 1914. Her commander, Fregattenkapitän Max Looff, received word of imminent hostilities from the Admiralstab via the wireless station in Nauen on July 31 and immediately put to sea so as not to be trapped in Dar es Salaam by the cruisers of the Royal Navy's Cape Squadron. As *Königsberg* left Dar es Salaam Looff spotted the British cruisers *Astraea*, *Hyacinth*, and *Pegasus* sitting off the harbor entrance and they proceeded to shadow the German warship. That evening, *Königsberg* entered a squall and immediately changed course at full speed, quickly losing her older and slower pursuers. For the next few days Looff sat off Mafia Island, around 100 miles south of Dar es Salaam off the mouth of the Rufiji River, awaiting news from Europe. On August 5, Looff sailed northwards, intent on being off the mouth of the Red Sea when war began, but later that day he received a wireless message reporting the Allied declarations of war on Germany. On August 6, off the coast of Oman, *Königsberg* captured her only merchant prize, the 6,601-ton British freighter *City of Winchester*. Looff then sailed towards the northern coast of Madagascar to raid on the sea lanes used by French merchantmen, but none were to be found.

B

KARLSRUHE

Fregattenkapitän Köhler had several advantages that led to *Karlsruhe*'s successful raiding career. He had access to a relatively ample supply of coal from Etappenschiffe that were able to base and operate out of a large number of neutral ports where they could purchase coal and provisions. He also received additional supplies of coal from captured enemy colliers and put prize crews aboard three of these, turning them into auxiliaries under the German ensign: *Strathroy* was converted into *Kohlendampfer KD1*, *Indrani* into *Kohlendampfer KD 2*, and *Farn* into *Kohlendampfer KD 3* – and on October 11, 1914, *Kohlendampfer KD-3* captured a prize of her own, the British 3,053-ton freighter *Condor*. *Karlsruhe* was able to use several remote anchorages as ersatz supply bases where Etappenschiffe could anchor and stay on station so *Karlsruhe* could return when necessary to coal. Köhler and his colliers first used the Atol de Rocas around 200 miles off the Brazilian coast in late August and then moved to Lavendeira Reef just off the northern Brazilian coast which he used for almost two months. Finally *Karlsruhe* had the advantage of operating in a large and open area that made detection by the enemy difficult.

Königsberg firing on protected cruiser HMS *Pegasus* off Zanzibar on the morning of September 20, 1914.

LEFT
SMS *Königsberg* sailing out of Dar es Salaam harbor in German East Africa.

RIGHT
A unique reconnaissance photo taken from a British floatplane showing the Rufiji Delta and *Königsberg's* lair. *Königsberg* can be seen toward the upper right of the photo with smoke coming out of her second funnel. A German supply boat is in the center of the photo.

Königsberg eventually set course for the Rufiji Delta, entering the waterway on September 3; Looff needed a secluded anchorage to repair a damaged boiler, undertake routine maintenance, and coal. The Rufiji Delta had several channels deep and wide enough for *Königsberg* to navigate through and a supply and repair base was set up in the middle of a mangrove forest at the tiny customs station of Salale several miles upstream. On September 19 Looff learned from German coast watchers that a British cruiser had put into port at Zanzibar for repairs and he decided to attack her. *Königsberg* sailed out of the Rufiji in the early hours of September 20 and approached Zanzibar undetected. Looff closed to within 7,000 meters of the stationary 2,740-ton protected cruiser HMS *Pegasus* and opened fire. Less than half an hour and over 300 10.5cm shells later, *Königsberg* departed the scene, leaving *Pegasus* a smoking wreck that capsized later that day. Unfortunately for the Germans, *Königsberg's* boilers were further damaged during the bombardment and Looff was immediately forced to return upriver to Salale for repairs. The British eventually learned the location of *Königsberg's* secret anchorage and blockaded her there until she was sunk in the delta on June 11, 1915, in a gun duel with two shallow-draft monitors, sent from Britain to destroy the cruiser in her lair (for the details of *Königsberg's* campaign in the Rufiji Delta see Plate C).

SMS *Leipzig*

Dimensions:	length: 364ft 9in
	beam: 43ft 8in
	draft: 18ft 5in
Displacement:	3,756 tons
Complement:	288
Armament:	ten 10.5cm SK L/40 guns, two located side-by-side fore, six amidships (three on each side), and two side-by-side aft; ten 37mm Maxim auto cannon; two 450mm torpedo tubes, underwater, one on each broadside
Machinery:	two triple expansion engines, coal-fired by ten marine boilers, generating up to 11,750 IHP and turning two screws at a maximum speed of 22 knots
Maximum Range:	4,690 nautical miles at 12 knots
Protection:	conning tower: 3.9in on the sides, ¾in on the roof
	armored deck: 3.1in amidships tapering to ¾in on both ends with 2in of sloped armor on the sides
	gun shields: 2in
Coal Capacity:	860 tons
Builder:	AG Weser of Bremen (1906)

Leipzig was on station in the port of Mazatlán on the Mexican Pacific coast, protecting German interests in the midst of the Mexican Revolution, when the war began in Europe. After a fruitless attempt to raid British shipping off the American coast, *Leipzig*'s commander, Fregattenkapitän Johannes Haun, received orders from the Admiralstab on September 3, 1914, to conduct commerce raiding operations along the Pacific coast of South America. *Leipzig* headed south and took on coal from two colliers from Etappe San Francisco. On September 11 *Leipzig* took her first prize, the 6,542-ton British tanker *Elsinore*, off Puerto Vallarta. On September 25 Haun stopped and sank the 3,763-ton British freighter *Bankfields* off Guayaquil. Haun picked up a wireless message from the Admiralstab on October 1 instructing *Leipzig* to meet up with the cruiser *Dresden*. Haun

SMS *Leipzig* in the floating dry dock at Tsingtau.

decided to set a rendezvous with *Dresden* at Easter Island and on October 3 learned from a wireless message from *Dresden* that the Kreuzergeschwader was also headed to Easter Island. *Leipzig* arrived at Easter Island on October 14, meeting *Scharnhorst, Gneisenau, Nürnberg, Dresden,* and several supply ships. On October 18 the reconstituted Kreuzergeschwader sailed east and on November 1 fought the battle of Coronel. *Leipzig* and *Dresden* briefly engaged the British light cruiser *Glasgow* before she escaped into the night but otherwise played little part in the battle. On November 2, while sailing to a coaling rendezvous, *Leipzig* captured the 3,120-ton French bark *Valentine* (coal offloaded). *Leipzig* rejoined the Kreuzergeschwader on November 18 and eight days later Spee's force made its break for the Atlantic.

On December 2 Haun captured the 1,844-ton British bark *Drummuir*. In the ensuing battle of the Falkland Islands on December 8, after Spee ordered his light cruisers to scatter, *Leipzig* drove off *Glasgow* with accurate fire but was then targeted by the armored cruiser *Cornwall*. The two ships engaged each other for almost three hours and *Glasgow* later rejoined the fight. Although *Leipzig*'s fire was accurate, her 10.5cm shells did little damage to the more heavily protected *Cornwall*; after expending all of his 10.5cm ammunition and attempting a torpedo attack, Haun ordered *Leipzig* to be scuttled. She capsized quickly, taking all but 18 of her crew with her.

C

KÖNIGSBERG

Königsberg spent the majority of her wartime career bottled up in the Rufiji Delta in German East Africa but she served as a solitary "Fleet-in-Being" that the British could not ignore. After sinking HMS *Pegasus*, *Königsberg* was laid up for weeks at her lair at Salale; one of her boilers was too heavily damaged for repairs on site and it had to be sent to the naval workshop in Dar es Salaam via a sledge and a thousand native laborers. A defense force, the *Abteilung Delta*, made up of sailors and Askaris, was established to patrol the delta and a number of lookout posts and gun emplacements, armed with 37mm guns from *Königsberg* and connected by field telephones to the cruiser, were set up. Thus any British approach would be reported and *Königsberg* would be able to train her 10.5cm guns on any intruder with fire being directed by the lookout posts. In the meantime the British were busy searching for the phantom cruiser but on October 19, 1914, a boarding party from the British light cruiser *Chatham* discovered *Königsberg*'s location from documents captured aboard a German liner. On October 30 *Chatham* sailed up the channel leading to *Königsberg*'s purported location and eventually a lookout spotted two ship's masts in the distance just above the treetops. *Chatham*, joined by the light cruisers *Dartmouth* and *Weymouth*, attempted to shell *Königsberg* from as far inland as their draft would allow them but Fregattenkapitän Looff simply moved *Königsberg* further upriver and out of range.

The British attempted to penetrate the delta on foot and in small boats with marines and sailors but each time they were beaten back by the forces of the Abteilung Delta or *Königsberg*'s shore-mounted gun batteries. Looff, however, was in no position to undertake offensive action for by December many of his sailors were struck down with malaria and he was forced to release a large number of his crew for service in Oberstleutnant Paul von Lettow-Vorbeck's colonial army, the Schutztruppe. The situation remained a stalemate for the next six months. The course of events in the delta suddenly changed on June 3, 1915, when two shallow-draft monitors armed with two 6in guns and two 4.7in howitzers, HMS *Mersey* and HMS *Severn*, arrived from Britain with the sole purpose of destroying *Königsberg*. After an abortive attempt on June 6, *Mersey* and *Severn* sailed up the Rufiji on June 11 and after a two-hour bombardment, aided by a spotter aircraft equipped with a wireless set, the monitors fired on *Königsberg* until the cruiser's guns went silent and she suffered an ammunition explosion. Twenty minutes before the British bombardment ended, *Königsberg* was scuttled by her crew. Later, her 10.5cm guns were salvaged from the wreck, taken to Dar es Salaam, and placed on makeshift gun carriages, serving with the Schutztruppe for much of the rest of the war.

THE LINERS

SMS *Berlin*

Dimensions:	length: 610ft 3in
	beam: 69ft 10in
	draft: 28ft 3in
Displacement:	23,700 tons
Complement:	310 (estimated)
Armament:	two 10.5cm SK L/40 guns, one fore and one aft; six 37mm QF guns, distributed along the promenade deck; 200 mines
Machinery:	two vertical quadruple expansion engines, coal-fired by seven boilers, generating up to 16,000 IHP and turning two screws up to 19 knots
Maximum Range:	4,000 nautical miles at 10 knots
Coal Capacity:	4,000 tons
Builder:	AG Weser of Bremen (1908)
Owner:	Norddeutscher Lloyd

LEFT
SMS *Berlin* anchored near Trondheim after her minelaying cruise in October 1914.

RIGHT
The dreadnought HMS *Audacious* sinking on October 27, 1914, after striking a mine laid by *Berlin* off the northern Irish coast.

Berlin was not one of the designated reserve auxiliaries, but the Kaiserliche Marine determined that she could be useful as a cruiser/minelayer and she was outfitted as such beginning in August. Minelaying rails were mounted on her afterdeck and she was equipped to carry up to 200 mines. Repainted to look like a British liner, *Berlin* sailed out of Bremerhaven on October 16, 1914, with orders to proceed to the western coast of Scotland and lay a minefield off the Clyde Estuary. Hugging the Norwegian coast up the North Sea, she passed around Scotland through the Faroes Gap and reached the northern coast of Ireland on the evening of October 22. Her commander, Kapitän zur See Hans Pfundheller, decided not to proceed towards the Clyde due to a large amount of enemy wireless traffic in the area and instead laid a minefield across a shipping lane between Tory Island and Lough Swilly on the northern Irish coast. *Berlin* departed the area on the morning of the 23rd and headed to the northeast, intent on disrupting the shipping lanes between Great Britain and Archangel in Russia. For two weeks Pfundheller cruised the northern waters but encountered nothing and on November 17, with her coal supply nearly exhausted, *Berlin* sailed into Trondheim, Norway. Pfundheller, who feared being intercepted by the British in the North Sea, agreed to intern *Berlin* and his crew to the Norwegian authorities the following day.

While *Berlin*'s guns accounted for no enemy vessels, her mines were responsible for one of the worst British warship losses of the war. Unknown to Pfundheller a number of heavy units of the Grand Fleet were based in Lough Swilly in late October due to a U-boat scare at Scapa Flow. On October 27 the 23,780-ton super-dreadnought HMS *Audacious* ran into one of *Berlin*'s mines and capsized 12 hours later; *Audacious* was the largest ship sunk by the Hilfskreuzer during the war. The 5,363-ton British freighter *Manchester Commerce* was also lost to a mine from *Berlin* on the same day.

SMS *Cap Trafalgar*

Dimensions:	length: 610ft 3in
	beam: 69ft 10in
	draft: 27ft 3in
Displacement:	23,640 tons
Complement:	319
Armament:	two 10.5cm SK L/35 guns, one mounted just aft of the forecastle to port and the other on the poop deck to starboard; six 37mm QF guns, distributed along the promenade deck
Machinery:	two vertical triple expansion engines and one low-pressure exhaust turbine, coal-fired by 14 boilers, generating up to 15,900 IHP and turning three screws at 17.8 knots
Maximum Range:	7,100 nautical miles at 15 knots
Coal Capacity:	5,100 tons
Builder:	AG Vulcan of Hamburg (1914)
Owner:	Hamburg-Südamerikanischen Dampfschiffahrtsgesellschaft

Cap Trafalgar was moored in Buenos Aires when the war began and she was ordered to sea on August 15 as she was a designated reserve auxiliary cruiser. Unable to fully coal in Buenos Aires she headed for Montevideo where she completed filling her bunkers on August 23. She then sailed north to Ilha da Trindade and arrived there on August 28 for a prearranged rendezvous with the gunboat *Eber* and the Etappenschiff *Steiermark*, both of which had sailed from Lüderitz in German Southwest Africa with orders to arm the liner. *Eber* transferred her armament and most of her crew to *Cap Trafalgar* and the gunboat's captain, Korvettenkapitän Julius Wirth, assumed command of the auxiliary cruiser. During her conversion, *Cap Trafalgar*'s third funnel was removed and her remaining two were painted red with black tops in an effort to make her look like a British Cunard liner from a distance. On September 4 Wirth headed for the sea lanes off eastern South America but encountered no enemy vessels over the next several days. With coal stocks already running low he arranged to meet three Etappenschiffe at Ilha da Trindade and arrived there on the evening of September 13. The following day the British armed merchant cruiser *Carmania* appeared and *Cap Trafalgar* was sunk in an ensuing gunnery duel (for details of this battle see Plate D).

Hamburg-Südamerikanischen Dampfschiffahrtsgesellschaft poster showing *Cap Trafalgar* as she looked prior to her conversion into a Hilfskreuzer.

SMS *Cormoran*

Dimensions:	length: 341ft 2in
	beam: 44ft 11in
	draft: 19ft
Displacement:	7,250 tons
Complement:	347
Armament:	eight 10.5cm SK L/35 guns, two on the forecastle, two in front of the bridge, two aft of the superstructure, and two on the poop deck
Machinery:	one vertical triple expansion engine, coal-fired by four boilers, generating up to 4,750 IHP and turning one screw up to 14 knots
Maximum Range:	13,500 nautical miles at 14 knots
Coal Capacity:	2,500 tons
Builder:	Schichau AG of Elbing (1909)
Owner:	Dobroflot (Russian Volunteer Fleet)

Cormoran began the war as the Russian *Ryazan* and ironically was the first enemy merchant vessel captured at sea by the Kaiserliche Marine's commerce raiders. She was stopped by *Emden* in the Straits of Tsushima on August 4 and taken to Tsingtau. Although she lacked the requirements set out for auxiliary cruisers before the war, she was converted into a Hilfskreuzer by arming her with eight 10.5cm guns taken from the old gunboat *Cormoran*. The *Ryazan* was also given the crew and name of the gunboat and sailed out of Tsingtau on August 10 to escort a group of colliers to the Marshall Islands. From there the newly christened *Cormoran*, under the command of Korvettenkapitän Adalbert Zuckschwerdt, was dispatched to raid merchant shipping off Australia on August 30. For two weeks she cruised the seas of the Bismarck Archipelago and the eastern Netherlands East Indies without coming across any enemy merchantmen.

CAP TRAFALGAR

Cap Trafalgar had the shortest career of the Hilfskreuzer, lasting only ten days. She is historically significant, however, because she was involved in the only sea battle between two armed ocean liners. On the morning of September 14, 1914, *Cap Trafalgar* was anchored off the Ilha da Trindade in the company of the Etappenschiffe *Eleonore Woerman*, *Pontos*, and *Berwind*. As the German crews were transferring coal from *Pontos* to *Cap Trafalgar* smoke was spotted on the horizon to the northeast at 1055hrs; it was HMS *Carmania*, a 19,500-ton Cunard liner that had been converted into an armed merchant cruiser. Korvettenkapitän Wirth ordered the colliers to scatter and *Cap Trafalgar* proceeded to escape to the south. *Cap Trafalgar* was beginning to pull ahead of her pursuer but at around noon she turned around toward *Carmania*, which opened fire a few minutes later.

For the next hour and a half the liners did battle; *Carmania* had a heavier armament of eight 4.7in guns but *Cap Trafalgar*'s gunnery was more precise. *Cap Trafalgar*'s gunners' primary target was *Carmania*'s bridge, which was obliterated, but a number of hits that *Cap Trafalgar* took below the waterline, causing a list to starboard, proved to be fatal to the German ship. At 13:30 *Cap Trafalgar* broke off the fight and Wirth set course for Ilha da Trindade, hoping to beach his heavily damaged and listing ship but to no avail; 20 minutes later *Cap Trafalgar* capsized and went to the bottom, having failed to sink a single Allied merchantman during her brief career. Her survivors were picked up by the German colliers and taken to Buenos Aires. The battle between *Cap Trafalgar* and *Carmania* had greater strategic significance for the British than the Germans. *Carmania* only just managed to survive the battle herself, having been hit around 80 times. The damage sustained by *Carmania* compelled the Royal Navy to pull the most valuable British liners (particularly *Aquitania* and *Mauretania*) from armed merchant cruiser service. These liners served in a much more important role as troop carriers, transporting hundreds of thousands of British, Imperial and American troops to France later in the war.

SMS *Cormoran* lying at anchor off Guam during her long internment.

Cormoran was plagued by poor fuel consumption and as a result burned through her coal stores quickly. On September 23 Zuckschwerdt put into the tiny port of Alexishafen in Kaiser Wilhelmsland (eastern New Guinea), expecting to rendezvous with an Etappenschiff. Two days later he learned from enemy wireless intercepts that the Australians had landed at Friedrich-Wilhelm-Hafen, only 15½ miles to the south. Zuckschwerdt immediately put to sea, narrowly avoiding the battlecruiser *Australia* and the French armored cruiser *Montcalm*, and escaped north to the German island of Yap. There he recruited the crew of the survey vessel *Planet* as naval infantry and planned to retake Friedrich-Wilhelm-Hafen, and her valuable coal supply, after the Allied warships had departed. *Cormoran* approached Friedrich-Wilhelm-Hafen on October 5 only to discover that *Montcalm* was still in port and so Zuckschwerdt headed back towards Yap. On the evening of the 8th, *Cormoran* approached Yap but came out of a fog bank only about 150 yards from the 19,372-ton Japanese battleship *Satsuma*; the Japanese had taken the island the day before. Fortunately visibility was poor and the Japanese did not spot *Cormoran*, which beat a hasty retreat back into the fog bank. With the misfortune of being in an area of heavy enemy naval activity with a slow vessel, Zuckschwerdt set course for the isolated anchorage of Lamutrik in the western Caroline Islands. With her coal supply nearly exhausted *Cormoran* remained at Lamutrik for two months while Zuckschwerdt sent a small party of officers aboard a small cutter to the American island of Guam to purchase coal or arrange a rendezvous with an Etappenschiff. On December 12, after no news from Guam, Zuckschwerdt learned from natives that the Japanese were approaching from the west and the following day *Cormoran* sailed for Guam, arriving on the 14th. Zuckschwerdt was informed by the American governor that he would only be permitted 100 tons of coal and, realizing that he had nowhere to go, interned his ship and crew.

Interned German sailors aboard *Cormoran* celebrating Christmas in 1915. *Cormoran* and her crew sat dormant at Guam until April 7, 1917, when the United States declared war on Germany. That day the Germans scuttled their ship and Korvettenkapitän Zuckschwerdt and his men became the first German prisoners-of-war taken by the Americans.

SMS *Kaiser Wilhelm der Grosse*

Dimensions:	length: 654ft 6in
	beam: 65ft 11in
	draft: 27ft 7in
Displacement:	24,300 tons
Complement:	584
Armament:	six 10.5cm SK L/40 guns, two located on each side of the forecastle, two in front of the bridge, and two just in front of the poop deck; two 37mm QF on each side of the promenade deck
Machinery:	two vertical triple expansion engines, coal-fired by 14 boilers, generating up to 28,000 IHP and turning two screws up to 22.5 knots
Maximum Range:	5,000 nautical miles at 18 knots
Coal Capacity:	4,550 tons
Builder:	AG Vulcan of Stettin (1897)
Owner:	Norddeutscher Lloyd

Kaiser Wilhelm der Grosse was the oldest German liner designated for Hilfskreuzer service but her well-worn engines could still make over 20 knots. She was also the only first-line Hilfskreuzer in home waters when the war began and she was armed in late July. Painted black and dark grey, she was ordered out of Bremerhaven on the morning of August 4 under the command of Fregattenkapitän Max Reymann. *Kaiser Wilhelm der Grosse* sailed up the North Sea, swung far to the north, and broke out into the Atlantic via the Denmark Strait on August 7. That day she sank her first prize, the 225-ton British trawler *Tubal Cain*. Reyman had orders to raid British shipping around the Azores and Canary Islands; it was estimated that she could steam at 12 knots for roughly 11 days before she would have to take on coal so a rendezvous with Etappenschiffe somewhere southeast of the Azores was arranged prior to departure. On August 12 *Kaiser Wilhelm der Grosse* came across the Italian liner *Il Piedmonte* southwest of the Azores and, being a neutral vessel with no contraband of war aboard, Reyman was forced to let her go; as the raider's presence was now known to the Italians, Reyman assumed it was only a matter of time before the British would learn of his activity.

Kaiser Wilhelm der Grosse finally came upon four British merchantmen on August 15 and 16. Two of the prizes, the 6,762-ton *Galician* and 15,044-ton *Arlanza*, were mail steamers carrying passengers, including women and children, and as a result Reyman let them go after the wireless antennas aboard both ships were disabled. The other two prizes, the 7,392-ton *Kaipara* and 3,066-ton *Nyanga*, were freighters and were sunk. On August 17 *Kaiser Wilhelm der Grosse* put into the small Spanish anchorage of Rio de Oro in North Africa and waited for the arrival of his Etappenschiffe. Reyman told the Spanish authorities that the liner

SMS *Kaiser Wilhelm der Grosse* under attack from HMS *Highflyer* in Rio de Oro on August 26, 1914.

Kaiser Wilhelm der Grosse lying on her port side after her battle with *Highflyer*. Ironically most of the shells the British fired had simply passed through the liner's thin sides without exploding and it was her scuttling charges that ultimately caused her to capsize.

was experiencing engine trouble and would be there for several days. As Reyman and his crew were still wearing Norddeutscher Lloyd uniforms, the Spanish did not suspect the ship of being a raider. On August 24–25, three colliers arrived at Rio de Oro and *Kaiser Wilhelm der Grosse* was in the process of coaling when a British warship was spotted on the horizon just after noon on August 26; it was the 5,650-ton protected cruiser HMS *Highflyer*. When ordered to surrender by the British, Reyman claimed to be a merchant ship under the protection of Spanish neutrality but *Highflyer* opened fire. Reyman ordered the colliers to scatter and engaged the British cruiser. Roughly an hour and a half later *Kaiser Wilhelm der Grosse* exhausted her supply of ammunition and Reyman had the vessel scuttled.

SMS *Kronprinz Wilhelm*

Dimensions:	length: 663ft 4in; beam: 66ft 3in; draft: 27ft 10in
Displacement:	24,900 tons
Complement:	503
Armament:	two 8.8cm SK L/35 guns, both mounted starboard on the forecastle
Machinery:	two vertical quadruple expansion engines, coal-fired by 16 boilers, generating up to 36,000 IHP and turning two screws up to 23.3 knots
Maximum Range:	4,800 nautical miles at 18 knots
Coal Capacity:	4,880 tons
Builder:	AG Vulcan of Stettin (1901)
Owner:	Norddeutscher Lloyd

Kronprinz Wilhelm was in New York on August 2, 1914 when she received orders from the Etappe New York commander to immediately coal, provision, and to proceed to sea to rendezvous with a cruiser and be armed for raiding duties. On August 6, north of the Bahamas, *Kronprinz Wilhelm* met *Karlsruhe*, which gave the liner two guns and ammunition, and the cruiser's navigator, Kapitänleutnant Paul Thierfelder, took command of the new Hilfskreuzer. After her meeting with *Karlsruhe* was cut short by HMS *Suffolk*, *Kronprinz Wilhelm* escaped across the Central Atlantic to the Azores where it met a collier from Etappe Westafrika on August 17. After taking on a full load of coal Thierfelder proceeded south to raid the

E   KRONPRINZ WILHELM

Kronprinz Wilhelm operated in the same area as *Karlsruhe* and enjoyed similar success. Kapitänleutnant Thierfelder found the sea lanes of the Southern Atlantic off Brazil to be fruitful raiding territory with the vastness of the area minimizing the threat of detection by the British, even for a large German liner. Thierfelder was able to take advantage of the large number of Etappenschiffe in the South Atlantic but arranged for coaling meetings to be made at sea after learning about the ambush of *Cap Trafalgar* at Ilha da Trindade while she was coaling. Coaling at sea was much more laborious and difficult, however, and *Kronprinz Wilhelm* spent most of September 1914 having her large bunkers filled from colliers from Etappe Brasilien and La Plata. Nevertheless *Kronprinz Wilhelm* was able to remain at large, taking coal from prizes and routinely being supplied at sea by Etappenschiffe, and remained a phantom to the Royal Navy. Thierfelder also successfully used Etappenschiffe as scouts and reconnaissance reports from German ships in neutral ports as *Karlsruhe* had done.

shipping lanes off Brazil, taking his first prize, the 2,846-ton British freighter *Indian Prince* on September 4. On October 7 *Kronprinz Wilhelm* captured the 8,529-ton British freighter *La Correntina*, which offered the raider a unique set of prizes. *La Correntina* had been armed with two 4.7in guns but had no ammunition; Thierfelder's crew promptly removed the guns from the freighter before scuttling her in the hopes that they might later acquire ammunition for them. Thierfelder then raided along the Brazilian coast as far south as the Rio de la Plata until December, after which he cruised back and forth across the sea lanes of the central Atlantic between Cabo de São Roque off northeastern Brazil and the Cape Verde Islands for the next three months.

From October 28 to March 27, 1915, *Kronprinz Wilhelm* captured the following prizes (British unless otherwise noted): October 28 – 2,183-ton French bark *Union* (coal offloaded); November 21 – 2,063 French bark *Anne de Bretagne*; December 4 – 3,814-ton collier *Bellevue* (coal offloaded) and 4,803-ton French freighter *Mont Agel*; December 28 – 3,486-ton collier *Hemisphere* (coal offloaded); January 10, 1915 – 4,419-ton freighter *Potaro* (prize crew placed aboard and served as a scout until scuttled on January 30); January 14 – 251-ton schooner *Wilfred M* and 7,364-ton freighter *Highland Brae*; February 5 – 2,280-ton Norwegian bark *Semantha* (carrying British cargo); February 22 – 4,583-ton collier *Chasehill* (coal offloaded and released with prisoners on March 9); February 23 – 6,600-ton French steamer *Guadeloupe*; March 24 – 3,207-ton freighter *Tamar*; March 27 – 3,824-ton freighter *Coleby*. By the end of March some members of *Kronprinz Wilhelm's* crew were beginning to suffer from scurvy and beriberi due to a longtime lack of fresh fruits and vegetables; furthermore coal was beginning to run low and the ship's hull was badly fouled and damaged in areas from coaling

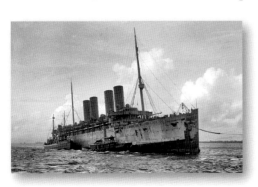

on the high seas and ramming down captured vessels (a tactic occasionally employed by Thierfelder due to low supplies of ammunition). Opting to attempt repairs or seek internment, Thierfelder decided to make a run for Newport News, Virginia at full speed and in the process burned up the last of his coal. On the evening of April 10 *Kronprinz Wilhelm* made a dash into Chesapeake Bay, steaming undetected between two patrolling British cruisers, and on the following morning anchored alongside another Hilfskreuzer, *Prinz Eitel Friedrich*, in the Norfolk Navy Yard.

SMS *Prinz Eitel Friedrich*

Dimensions:	length: 502ft 11in
	beam: 55ft 5in
	draft: 23ft 4in
Displacement:	16,000 tons
Complement:	402
Armament:	four 10.5cm SK L/35 guns, two mounted side-by-side on the forecastle and two side-by-side on the poop deck; six 8.8cm SK L/40 guns, four mounted ahead of the bridge (two on each side) and two just aft of the superstructure (one on each side); 12 37mm guns, distributed around the promenade deck
Machinery:	two vertical quadruple expansion engines, fired by four boilers, generating up to 7,000 IHP and turning two screws up to 17 knots
Maximum Range:	10,000 nautical miles at 14 knots
Coal Capacity:	6,000 tons
Builder:	AG Vulcan of Stettin (1904)
Owner:	Norddeutscher Lloyd

On July 31, 1914, *Prinz Eitel Friedrich* was serving on Norddeutscher Lloyd's Far Eastern route and received orders to immediately proceed to Tsingtau for conversion into a Hilfskreuzer. Arriving there on August 2 she was armed with guns taken from the old gunboats *Luchs* and *Tiger*. Her crew also came from these and other river gunboats and Korvettenkapitän Max Thierichens of *Luchs* was appointed her commander. She departed Tsingtau on August 6 and escorted several colliers to the Kreuzergeschwader in the Marshall Islands. Along with *Cormoran*, Spee dispatched *Prinz Eitel Freidrich* initially to raid the shipping lines off Australia and in the South Seas but a lack of merchant shipping and Australian and Japanese campaigns against Germany's Pacific colonies made the area a fruitless and dangerous place for raider operations. Thierichens decided to abandon the area and proceeded east in order to obtain coal from the nearest source, Etappe Valparaiso. On October 27, Thierichens received instructions to rendezvous with Spee's colliers at the isolated island of Mas a Fuera, 400 miles west off the Chilean coast, and escort them to Valparaiso; he was then to remain off Valparaiso, serving as a scout for the Kreuzergeschwader. Spee departed for the Falklands on November 15 but ordered *Prinz Eitel Friedrich* to remain in the area and transmit false wireless signals, hoping to deceive the British into thinking the Kreuzergeschwader was still off the western coast of South America.

The raider took her first prize on December 5, the 5,067-ton British freighter *Charcas*. After observing heavy British wireless traffic for several days, *Prinz Eitel Friedrich* intercepted wireless messages on December 10 confirming the destruction of the Kreuzergeschwader. Short on coal, Thierichens thought his raiding days were over but on that same day fortune intervened; the 2,207-ton French bark *Jean*, carrying 3,000 tons

SMS *Prinz Eitel Friedrich* after being interned in the United States. Note the two 10.5cm SK L/35 guns mounted on the poop deck.

of coal, sailed right into the path of the German raider. Thierichens put a prize crew aboard *Jean* and both ships proceeded to Easter Island where *Prinz Eitel Friedrich* could fill her bunkers. En route the 1,784-ton British bark *Kidalton* was captured and sunk. On December 24 *Prinz Eitel Friedrich* anchored in Cook Bay on Easter Island and took on coal for the next week.

On January 6, 1915, Thierichens raised anchor and headed for the shipping lanes of the South Atlantic after learning of heavy enemy merchant activity there from wireless intercepts; during *Prinz Eitel Friedrich*'s time at Easter Island, Thierichens had sent a small detachment with a wireless transmitter to the top of the island to listen in on enemy wireless traffic. Thierichens charted a course far to the south of Cape Horn into Antarctic waters to avoid Royal Navy patrols and on January 24 he set a northward course into the mid-Atlantic. Over the next month, *Prinz Eitel Friedrich* took eight prizes: January 26 – 1,315-ton Russian bark *Isabel Browne*; January 27 – French 2,196-ton bark *Pierre Loti* and American 3,374-ton bark *William P. Frye* (the German government was later forced to pay damages to the United States for the sinking of this neutral vessel, although it was carrying cargo bound for Great Britain); January 28 – 2,195-ton French bark *Jacobsen*; February 12 – 1,421-ton British bark *Invercoe*; February 18 – 3,605-ton British steamer *Mary Ada Short*; February 19 – 6,629-ton French steamer *Floride*, February 20 – 3,630-ton British steamer *Willeby*. By late February *Prinz Eitel Friedrich* had 350 prisoners aboard with dwindling food and water supplies. Although he had just enough coal to make an attempt to return to Germany, Thierichens judged the risk to be too great as enemy wireless traffic increased the further north he sailed. Thierichens opted for the safety of a neutral American port and in the early morning hours of March 10 sailed into the Chesapeake Bay, requesting a pilot to take him into Newport News, Virginia. There the American authorities granted Thierichens a stay of four weeks and dry-dock facilities to make repairs to the liner's worn engines and fouled hull but after the arrival of three British and one French cruiser off the Chesapeake Bay, Thierichens, on orders from Berlin, handed over *Prinz Eitel Friedrich* to the Americans for internment on April 9, 1915.

THE FREIGHTERS

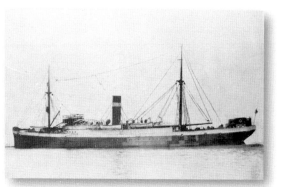

The first phase of Hilfskreuzer commerce raiding in the war ended on April 26, 1915 when *Kronprinz Wilhelm* was interned in the United States. All of the other Hilfskreuzer had been sunk or interned and the Etappendienst was for the most part expended through a combination of Etappenschiffe being captured or sunk at sea by the Allies or interned in neutral nations whose attitudes towards the war at sea had turned against Germany. The large amounts of coal consumed by the converted liners and the difficulties keeping them supplied meant that long-term operations against Allied commerce simply could not be maintained. However, it must be noted that the Hilfskreuzer offensive and Etappendienst had been designed for a war that was supposed to last for several months, not years; like the Army and its over-reliance upon the Schlieffen Plan, Germany's prewar naval planners never anticipated a protracted conflict and were strategically bankrupt when faced with that reality. With that being taken into account, the liner Hilfskreuzer offensive and Etappendienst had achieved their short-term tactical goal of disrupting Allied trade and tying down Allied naval assets. Nevertheless, by the summer of 1915 the Admiralstab was desperate to undertake some form of offensive operations following the restrictions placed on the operations of the High Seas Fleet by the Kaiser after the disaster at the battle of Dogger Bank and the abrupt end of the first U-boat campaign against enemy commerce due to political fallout from the sinking of *Lusitania*. The discussion of renewed Hilfskreuzer operations began again in late 1915/early 1916.

In the spring of 1915 the German High Command, about to launch an offensive on the Eastern Front, asked the Admiralstab about the possibility of laying mines off Russia's White Sea ports in an attempt to disrupt munitions shipments from Great Britain and France. The Admiralstab ordered the conversion of the 3,640-ton British freighter *Vienna* into a *Hilfsminenschiff* (auxiliary minelayer) for the task. It was assumed that as *Vienna* was a British vessel, it would be easier for her to run the British blockade of the North Sea than an easily recognizable German warship or liner; deception would be her defense rather than speed.

Rechristened SMS *Meteor* and placed under the command of Korvettenkapitän Wolfram von Knorr, *Meteor* headed into the North Sea on May 29, 1915, with a Zeppelin and U-boat scouting ahead for British warships. With this reconnaissance assistance *Meteor* successfully ran the British blockade, laid ten minefields (300 mines) off Arkhangel, and safely returned to Germany. Furthermore she captured three neutral cargo ships carrying Allied contraband on her return journey (she had been armed with two 8.8cm SK L/40 guns and later was equipped with two torpedo tubes). On August 6, Knorr took *Meteor* into the North Sea again to lay a minefield off northern Scotland. After laying her mines, *Meteor* ambushed and sank the British 1,520-ton armed boarding vessel *The Ramsey* with a torpedo on the evening of August 9. On her return to Germany *Meteor* was intercepted by British cruisers and scuttled to avoid capture; Knorr and his crew escaped to Germany aboard a passing Swedish vessel. While the career of *Meteor* was short-lived it demonstrated that an innocent-looking freighter, properly armed and manned, could pass through British blockade lines and successfully conduct mine and commerce warfare against the enemy. Furthermore it showed that a relatively expendable vessel with a smaller crew could undertake similar missions as valuable warships or expensive liners, offering the potential of a high return for a minimum investment.

Although *Meteor* was officially classified as a Hilfsminenschiff, several younger officers argued for the similar conversion of freighters into new *Frachtdampfer-*

The innocent-looking but lethal SMS *Möwe* (Bundesarchiv, Bild 134-B0354, photo: o.Ang)

SMS *Greif* had the shortest career of the Frachtdampfer-Hilfskreuzer. Converted in a similar way to *Möwe*, she entered the North Sea disguised as a Norwegian vessel on her first and only mission on February 27, 1916. Two days later she was intercepted by a British patrol but torpedoed the 15,831-ton armed merchant cruiser HMS *Alcantara* before being sunk herself.

Hilfskreuzer (freighter-auxiliary cruisers). Having smaller engines with less horsepower and lower speeds than liners, freighters consumed considerably less coal, which in turn gave them a much greater operating radius. Their cargo holds would allow them to carry extra coal, large amounts of supplies, a significant number of mines, and provide accommodation for numerous prisoners on long voyages – all without dependence upon the Etappendienst. Freighters would also be equipped with powerful wireless receivers in order to receive reports regarding Allied shipping changes or warship deployments from naval intelligence in Berlin via the Nauen transmitter. Finally, vessels selected for conversion had to resemble British-manufactured freighters and would be given various shades of paint and other materials which could be used to disguise them as vessels from Allied or neutral shipping lines while at sea. The Admiralstab was impressed enough by *Meteor*'s performance as an auxiliary minelayer that it ordered the conversion and arming of another freighter, *Möwe*, for minelaying missions in enemy waters. Korvettenkapitän Nikolaus Graf und Burggraf zu Dohna-Schlodien, commander of *Möwe*, oversaw her conversion into a minelayer but insisted that she be armed with several 15cm guns (experience from the earlier Hilfskreuzer campaign showed that the 10.5cm gun lacked the power needed to easily sink enemy vessels) and torpedo tubes as he intended to show that such a ship could be used for raiding enemy commerce. The Admiralstab had not ruled out the contingency to conduct commerce raiding with *Möwe* but left that decision to the discretion of her commander. However, raiding is exactly what Dohna-Schlodien intended to do and his subsequent success spurred the conversion of other freighters into Hilfskreuzer.

SMS *Möwe*

Dimensions:	length: 405ft 10in
	beam: 47ft 3in
	draft: 23ft 7in
Displacement:	9,800 tons
Complement:	235
Armament:	four 15cm SK L/45 guns, two mounted on each side of the forecastle; one 10.5cm SK L/45 gun mounted aft on the poop deck; four 500mm deck-mounted torpedo tubes, two hidden fore in front of the bridge, two hidden aft in front of the poop deck; 500 mines
Machinery:	one vertical triple expansion engine, fired by five boilers, generating up to 3,200 IHP and turning a single screw up to 13.3 knots
Maximum Range:	8,700 nautical miles at 12 knots
Coal Capacity:	3,440 tons
Builder:	J. C. Tecklenborg AG of Geestemünde (1914)
Owner:	F. Laeisz Reederei Norddeutscher Lloyd

On December 29, 1915, *Möwe*, formerly the banana boat *Pungo*, put to sea from Wilhelmshaven with orders to conduct minelaying operations in designated target zones of heavy Allied naval activity. With her northward route being scouted ahead by a U-boat, *Möwe* proceeded up the North Sea undetected and after rounding the Faroe Islands proceeded to lay 11 minefields (252 mines) off the northern coast of Scotland just west of the Pentland Firth on January 2, 1916. The 16,350-ton British pre-dreadnought *King Edward VII* fell victim to one of these mines on January 6. Dohna-Schlodien next proceeded west into the Atlantic and then turned south, making for the French coast. On the evening of January 9–10 he laid nine minefields (238 mines) off the Loire and Gironde estuaries; they would

Korvettenkapitän Dohna-Schlodien (center) on the bridge wing of *Möwe*. His aggressive raiding cruise through the Atlantic in the early months of 1916 convinced the Admiralstab to convert more freighters into Frachtdampfer-Hilfskreuzer. (Bundesarchiv, Bild 236-30, photo: o.Ang)

later account for two Spanish steamers totaling 4,844 tons. With his mines laid, Dohna-Schlodien decided to begin commerce raiding operations and set a course for the waters around the Canary Islands. Beginning on January 11, *Möwe* captured eight prizes off the Spanish coast and around the Canaries (all subsequent prizes are British unless otherwise noted): January 11 – 3,146-ton freighter *Farringford* and 3,687-ton collier *Corbridge* (retained as an auxiliary collier until later scuttled); January 13 – 3,627-ton collier *Dromonby*, 3,496-ton freighter *Author*, and 3,608-ton freighter *Trader*; January 15 – 3,035-ton freighter *Ariadne* and 7,781-ton liner *Appam* (prize crew put aboard and sent to the United States with prisoners); January 16 – 5,816-ton armed freighter *Clan Mactavish*. This rapid windfall of prizes had given Dohna-Schlodien over 200 prisoners and on January 17 he loaded them aboard the *Appam* and ordered the liner with a prize crew aboard to an American port; she arrived in Norfolk on February 1.

The German Dachshund sails the captured British liner *Appam* into the United States, flouting the might of the Royal Navy. Dohna-Schlodien captured the British liner *Appam* on January 15, 1916, loaded it with most of his prisoners, and sent it under the command of Leutnant Hans Berg to Norfolk, Virginia. The arrival of *Appam* with a load of prisoners was an embarrassment to the Royal Navy as it had falsely claimed that *Möwe* had been sunk. (Bundesarchiv, Bild 236-12, photo: o.Ang)

Möwe then proceeded to the northeastern Brazilian coast and between January 22 and February 9 took another five prizes: January 22 – 1,473-ton bark *Edinburgh*; February 4 – 4,322-ton Belgian collier *Luxembourg*; February 6 – 4,629-ton freighter *Flamenco*; February 8 – 3,300-ton collier *Westburn* (sent with a prize crew to Santa Cruz de Tenerife to offload prisoners and then used as an auxiliary collier until later scuttled); February 9 – 3,335-ton freighter *Horace*. By this time Dohna-Schlodien learned that the British were aware of his activities and decided to return to Germany. He set a northward course through the central Atlantic on February 9 and took two additional prizes on his route home: February 24 – 3,109-ton French freighter *Marconi*; February 25 – 3,471-ton freighter *Saxon Prince*. Cruising well to the west of Ireland *Möwe* entered the Denmark Strait on February 29 and after making a wide arc around the British Isles steamed down the Norwegian coast. After being escorted on her last leg by several squadrons of the High Seas Fleet, *Möwe* safely arrived in Wilhelmshaven on March 4. Throughout the summer months *Möwe*, temporarily renamed *Vineta* in order to throw off enemy surveillance of the now-famous raider, made several brief raiding cruises in the Skagerrak and Kattegat but only took a single prize: July 27 – 3,326-ton freighter *Eskimo* (taken to Swinemünde by a prize crew).

Dohna-Schlodien's operational foresight and dynamic initiative during *Möwe*'s first cruise provided tangible results that changed the Admiralstab's opinion regarding the potential of the Frachtdampfer-Hilfskreuzer concept. Other freighters were converted into Hilfskreuzer during the summer and autumn of 1916. While the strategy of unrestricted U-boat warfare for total victory against Britain was being hotly debated in the late autumn of 1916, the Admiralstab began a new offensive against British commerce using surface raiders, unleashing *Möwe*, *Wolf*, and *Seeadler*. *Möwe* sailed from Kiel on November 23 with three U-boats scouting a path through the British blockade for her. She broke out into the Atlantic through the Faroes Gap on November 26 and set a southward course. The month of December was particularly fruitful for *Möwe* as she took ten prizes: December 2 – 8,628-ton freighter *Voltaire*; December 4 – 2,586-ton Norwegian freighter *Hallbjørg* (carrying contraband cargo); December 6 – 9,792-ton freighter *Mount Temple*; December 8 – 152-ton bark *Duchess of Cornwall* and 3,852-ton freighter *King George*; December 9 – 4,235-ton freighter *Cambrian Range*; December 10 – 10,077-ton freighter *Georgic*; December 11 – 4,652-ton freighter *Yarrowdale* (prize crew put aboard and sent to Germany); December 12 – 4,992-ton collier *Saint Theodore* (retained as an auxiliary collier); December 18 – 5,415-ton freighter *Dramatist*.

As early as December 11 Dohna-Schlodien wanted to leave the main Atlantic shipping lanes as his presence had been betrayed by a Belgian Relief ship he was forced to release on December 4. He opted to sail for the sea lanes off Fernando de Noronha and northeastern Brazil but before he headed west he decided to outfit the collier *Saint Theodore* as a Hilfskreuzer. Command of the newly christened SMS *Geier*, armed with two spare 5.2cm SK L/55 guns from *Möwe*, was given to Kapitänleutnant Friedrich Wolf and she was dispatched to raid on December 28. *Geier* still retained plenty of coal to supply *Möwe* so she was ordered to rendezvous with her mother ship three weeks later in the mid-Atlantic. *Möwe* then headed for northeastern Brazil, taking the French barks *Nantes* (2,679 tons) and *Asnieres* (3,103 tons) on her way to the area on December 26, 1916 and January 2, 1917 respectively. In the waters off Fernando de Noronha *Möwe* captured an additional four vessels: January 5 – 3,708-ton Japanese freighter *Hudson Maru* (retained and released with prisoners on January 12); January 7 – 4,310-ton freighter *Radnorshire*; January 9 – 2,890-ton collier *Minieh*; January 10 – 4,461-ton freighter *Netherby Hall*.

Dohna-Schlodien set an eastward course after releasing his prisoners aboard *Hudson Maru* and met with *Geier* to coal on January 17. He then decided to raid the sea lanes approaching the Cape of Good Hope but after a week he came across no enemy merchantmen and so turned toward Ilha da Trindade for another coaling rendezvous with *Geier*. On February 13 the two vessels met and after the last of the coal from *Geier* was offloaded she was scuttled the following day (during her brief raiding career *Geier* captured two British sailing vessels totaling 1,442 tons). For the next week *Möwe* cruised east of Rio de Janeiro and took three prizes: February 15 – 8,423-ton collier *Brecknockshire*; February 16 – 4,766-ton freighter *French Prince* and 2,652-ton freighter *Eddie*. After scuttling *Eddie*, *Möwe* was sighted by the 13,329-ton armed merchant cruiser *Edinburgh Castle* but was able to successfully elude her pursuer in a squall.

The British freighter *Yarrowdale*, with a German prize crew aboard, steaming away from *Möwe*. Dohna-Schlodien sent her to Germany with over 500 prisoners and her original cargo of 117 American-made trucks and 3,200 tons of steel. *Yarrowdale* successfully ran the blockade and arrived in Swinemunde on December 31. She was later converted into the Hilfskreuzer SMS *Leopard* but was lost with all hands after a brief duel with two British warships northeast of the Faroe Islands on March 16, 1917. (Bundesarchiv, Bild 236-35, photo: o.Ang)

The escape from *Edinburgh Castle* made Dohna-Schlodien realize that his ship was in desperate need of maintenance and he decided to head for home, setting a northward course on February 18. As she made her way across the Atlantic sea lanes *Möwe* eliminated another six enemy vessels: February 24 – 2,926-ton freighter *Katherine*; March 4 – 3,061-ton freighter *Rhodanthe*; March 10 – 4,673-ton freighter *Esmeraldas* and 9,575-ton armed merchantman *Otaki* (sunk after taking over 30 hits in a running duel with *Möwe*); March 13 – 6,048-ton freighter *Demeterton*; March 14 – 5,524-ton freighter *Governor*. On March 17 *Möwe* again entered the Denmark Strait, desperate to reach Germany as she had nearly 600 prisoners aboard and supplies were running low. *Möwe* made an undetected run down the Norwegian coast and arrived in Kiel on March 22 to a hero's welcome.

SMS *Wolf*

Dimensions:	length: 442ft 11in
	beam: 56ft 1in
	draft: 25ft 11in
Displacement:	11,200 tons
Complement:	347
Armament:	seven 15cm SK L/40 guns, two hidden inside the forecastle, two hidden directly behind the forecastle, two hidden directly behind the superstructure, and one mounted aft; three 5.2cm SK L/55 guns kept in reserve; four 500mm deck-mounted torpedo tubes, two hidden fore in front of the bridge, two hidden aft in front of the poop deck; 465 mines
Machinery:	one vertical triple expansion engine, fired by three boilers, generating up to 2,800 IHP and turning a single screw up to 10.5 knots
Maximum Range:	42,000 nautical miles at 9 knots
Coal Capacity:	6,300 tons
Builder:	Flensburger Schiffbau-Gesellschaft of Flensburg (1913)
Owner:	Deutsche Dampfschiffahrtsgesellschaft Hansa

The freighter *Wachtfels* was selected for conversion into a Hilfskreuzer in late spring 1915 and was armed similarly to *Möwe*. On November 30, 1916, the rechristened *Wolf* secretly departed from Kiel, sailed up the North Sea without being detected, and broke out into the North Atlantic via the Denmark Strait in mid-December. Her commander, Korvettenkapitän Karl August Nerger, had orders to proceed to the Indian Ocean, lay minefields off a number of major British colonial ports, and then conduct commerce raiding prior to returning to Germany. For the next month *Wolf* made her way southward through the central Atlantic and laid five minefields (25 mines) off Cape Town on the evening of January 16, 1917, which later accounted for one Spanish and three British vessels (21,358 tons total). Two evenings later *Wolf* laid three minefields (29 mines) across the main shipping lanes to the east of the Cape and then headed east into the central Indian Ocean before turning north towards her next target, Colombo. During February 15–20, Nerger laid nine minefields (74 mines) in the sea lanes off Colombo and six off Bombay (110 mines); these minefields eventually claimed one Japanese and five British vessels of a total of 36,711 tons. On February 27 Nerger captured his first prize, the

A 15cm SK L/40 gun battery in front of a 500mm torpedo launcher on the deck of *Wolf*. Note the crewman in the middle of the photo with the headset; *Wolf* was equipped with a modern range finder and firing coordinates were relayed to gun batteries, giving the raider the same degree of fire control as a proper warship.

Wolf was similarly armed as *Möwe* but had a slower maximum speed of only 10.5 knots. As this was less than or equal to that of most enemy freighters Korvettenkapitän Nerger had the ingenious idea of equipping his ship with a reconnaissance floatplane: the Friedrichshafen FF.33e, named *Wölfchen* by the raider's crew, would be used to scout for enemy vessels and compel those sighted to heave to under threat of bombardment while the Hilfskreuzer caught up to capture the prizes. *Wölfchen* made a total of 56 flights during *Wolf*'s cruise and assisted in the capture of five enemy vessels. *Wölfchen* alone captured the 567-ton British schooner *Winslow* on June 16, 1917 when she dropped a bomb ahead of the vessel's bow, brazenly taxied up to the ship after landing, and the pilot, with pistol in hand, ordered the British captain to sail towards *Wolf*.

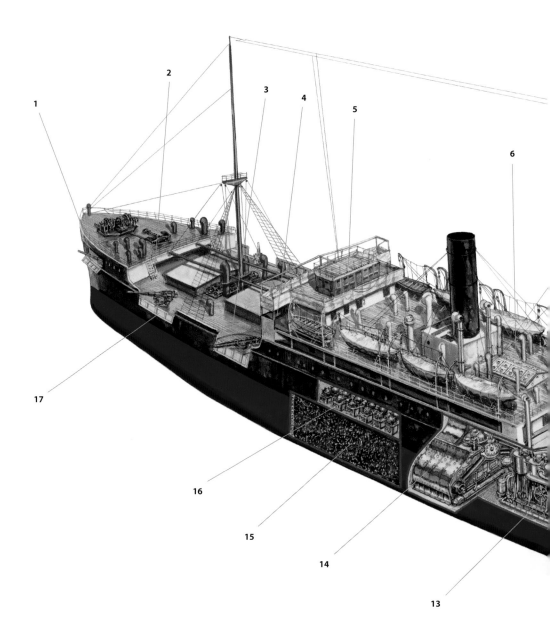

KEY

1. Forward hidden 15cm SK L/40 gun
2. 15cm SK L/40 gun
3. 500mm deck-mounted torpedo tube
4. Bridge
5. Wireless room
6. Boat deck
7. 500mm deck-mounted torpedo tube
8. Friedrichshafen FF.33e floatplane Wölfchen

9. 15cm SK L/40 gun disguised as a derrick
10. Mine storage and ammunition magazine
11. Prisoners hold
12. Coal bunker
13. Vertical triple expansion engine
14. Boilers
15. Coal bunker
16. Between-deck hold
17. Drop-down bulwark

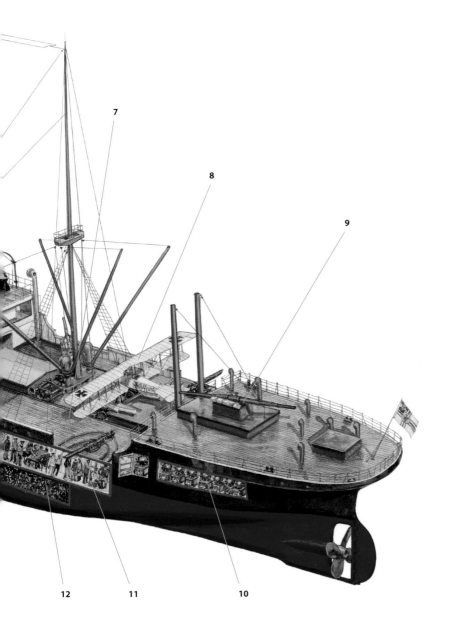

Korvettenkapitän Nerger equipped *Turritella* as an auxiliary minelayer with a single 5.2cm gun and 25 mines and dispatched Kapitänleutnant Iwan Brandes to lay a minefield off the mouth of the Red Sea. After laying her mines this new Hilfskreuzer, SMS *Iltis*, was scuttled on March 5, 1917, after being overtaken by a British warship.

Commander of the Kiel naval base, Admiral Gustav Bachmann, raising a cheer for Korvettenkapitän Nerger and the crew of *Wolf* after her return to Germany.

5,528-ton British tanker *Turritella*. This was the first time Nerger dispatched his secret weapon: a Friedrichshafen FF.33e floatplane named *Wölfchen* stored in one of the cargo holds which was used to conduct over-the-horizon scouting for *Wolf*. Nerger then took *Wolf* southward and turned east, sailing to the south of Australia and New Zealand. On this route *Wolf* captured three additional prizes: March 1 – 4,152-ton British freighter *Jumna*; March 11 – 3,509-ton British freighter *Wordsworth*; March 31 – 1,169-ton British bark *Dee*.

Over the next several weeks *Wolf* sailed an eastward course south of Australia and then, after rounding New Zealand from the east, proceeded to remote Raoul Island almost 700 miles northeast of New Zealand where she anchored on May 22 for a month of maintenance and repairs. Nerger had *Wölfchen* make scouting flights around the island to warn of the approach of any enemy vessels; *Wölfchen*'s efforts were rewarded on June 6 when she stopped the 3,947-ton British freighter *Wairuna* by dropping a bomb in front of her bow and *Wolf* steamed out to capture her. After repairs were complete and coal and supplies taken from *Wairuna*, Nerger left Raoul Island on June 22 and proceeded to lay 13 minefields (90 mines) in the sea lanes off New Zealand and Australia (these minefields claimed three British vessels totaling 17,793 tons). *Wolf* turned north on July 5 towards Fiji and then cruised westward through the Solomon Islands before anchoring off Waigeu Island in the Dutch East Indies on August 14 for another period of maintenance and resupply. During this period *Wolf* took three prizes: July 9 – 507-ton American bark *Beluga*; July 14 – 651-ton American schooner *Encore*; August 6 – 1,618-ton British steamer *Matunga* (coal offloaded). On August 26 Nerger continued eastward through the Dutch East Indies and after approaching Singapore from the Caremata Strait laid ten minefields (110 mines) off the northeastern approaches to the port on the evening of September 4–5. *Wolf* then sailed to the southeast, rounded the eastern coast of Java, and set a westward course across the Indian Ocean beginning on September 11.

The raider crossed the Indian Ocean, rounded the Cape of Good Hope on December 4, and crossed the Atlantic to arrive off Ilha da Trindade on December 18. Four additional prizes were taken during this time: September 17 – 6,557-ton Japanese steamer *Hitachi Maru*; November 10 – 4,648-ton Spanish collier *Igotz Mendi* (carrying contraband cargo and retained as an auxiliary collier); November 30 – 1,296-ton American bark *John H. Kirby*; December 15 – 2,192-ton French bark *Maréchal Davout*. From Ilha da Trindade Nerger turned south but then headed northward on December 30 and shortly after the New Year decided it was time to return to Germany. Over a year at sea had taken a toll on *Wolf*, with damage sustained during multiple coal transfers at sea, and by this time Nerger had a very large number of prisoners to accommodate; he had not released any prisoners throughout *Wolf*'s cruise so as to keep as much information from the enemy as possible. From December 31 to February 7, 1918, *Wolf* sailed up the Atlantic, along with *Igotz Mendi* which was being used to accommodate prisoners, sinking one last vessel along the way: January 4 – 2,050-ton Norwegian bark *Storebror* (technically neutral but sunk as Nerger did not want *Wolf*'s location to be reported). On February 7 *Wolf* and *Igotz Mendi* entered the Denmark Strait but were forced to head for the Faroes Gap due to pack ice. The two ships sailed undetected around the British Isles and down the Norwegian coast, making it safely into the Kattegat. *Igotz Mendi* ran aground on the Danish coast on February 24, her prize crew and passengers being interned in Denmark, but on the same day *Wolf* triumphantly sailed into Kiel.

SMS *Seeadler*

Dimensions:	length: 273ft 11in; beam: 38ft 9in; draft: 18ft
Displacement:	4,500 tons
Complement:	64
Armament:	two 10.5cm SK L/40 guns located fore on each side
Machinery:	one Usines Carels Frères SA four cylinder two-stroke diesel engine generating up to 900 IHP and turning a single screw up to 9 knots (16 knots achieved with full sail and engine)
Maximum Range:	40,000 nautical miles at 9 knots (greatly extended by using sails)
Builder:	Robert Duncan Company of Port Glasgow (1878)
Owner:	Harris-Irby Cotton Company of Boston

The American three-masted windjammer *Pass of Balmaha* was captured by a U-boat in the North Sea in the summer of 1915, bound with a contraband cargo for Arkhangel, and was sailed to Cuxhaven as a prize. She was put forward as a candidate for conversion into a Hilfskreuzer by a prewar Arctic explorer, Leutnant zur See Alfred Kling, who argued that the British would hardly expect a sailing ship to serve as a raider while a full-rigged windjammer would not have to rely upon coal for propulsion; as with the other Frachtdampfer, deception was to be this raider's main weapon.

The newly christened *Seeadler* began its cruise up the Norwegian coast on December 21, 1916, commanded by Korvettenkapitän Graf Felix von Luckner, and broke out into the Atlantic through the Faroes Gap. Luckner set a southward course through the central Atlantic and took his first two prizes just east of the Azores early into the New Year: January 9, 1917 – 3,268-ton British steamer *Gladys Royle*; January 10 – 3,095-ton British steamer *Lundy Island*. By late January *Seeadler* was just north of the equator in the central Atlantic and over the next several weeks took the majority of her prizes: January 21 – 2,199-ton French bark *Charles Gounod*; January 24 – 364-ton British schooner *Perce*; February 3 – 3,071-ton French bark *Antonin*; February 9 – 1,811-ton Italian sailing vessel *Buenos Ayres*; February 19 – 2,431 British bark *Pinmore*; February 26 – 1,953-ton British bark *British Yeoman*; February 27 – 2,200-ton French bark *La Rochefoucauld*; March 5 – 2,206-ton French bark *Dupleix*; March 11 – 3,609-ton British steamer *Horngarth*. On March 21 Luckner captured the 1,863-ton French bark *Cambronne* but released it to unload the 207 prisoners from his prior captures. The arrival of *Cambronne* in Rio de Janeiro on

The windjammer *Pass of Balmaha*, shown here before the war, which was converted into the unique Hilfskreuzer SMS *Seeadler* in 1916. (State Library of Victoria H91.250-281)

March 30 alerted the British to the presence of a new German raider and Luckner narrowly avoided a Royal Navy ambush around Cape Horn by sailing deep to the south into Antarctic waters before turning northwards into the Pacific.

By early May *Seeadler* was just south of Más á Tierra where *Dresden* met her end and Luckner set a course to the northwest. He had learned through wireless intercepts that the United States had entered the war against Germany and *Seeadler*'s last prizes were all American vessels taken in the central Pacific south of Hawaii: June 14 – 529-ton schooner *A.B. Johnson*; June 15 – 673-ton schooner *R.C. Slade*; July 8 – 731-ton schooner *Manila*. By this time *Seeadler* had been at sea for over half a year and Luckner decided to head for the remote Society Islands west of Tahiti in order to give his crew a rest and to clean the ship's fouled bottom. On July 31 *Seeadler* anchored at the atoll of Mopelia but on the morning of August 2 the ship's stern anchor lost her hold on the sea bottom and a combination of currents and a shifting wind drove her onto a coral reef; with her masts broken and hull split open she was a total wreck. Luckner and five of his crew sailed westward to the Fiji Islands in one of *Seeadler*'s launches, hoping to capture another ship, but after a harrowing voyage of over 2,000 miles they were captured by the British on Wakaya Island on September 21. The remaining crew on Mopelia signaled and captured a passing French sailing ship on August 23 and took her to Easter Island from where they were sent to mainland Chile for internment.

CONCLUSION

The effectiveness of the Kreuzerkrieg waged by the Kaiserliche Marine's surface raiders is still debated to this day. While Tirpitz's Risikogedanke ultimately failed, a concerted campaign against British commerce nearly succeeded in bringing the island nation to its knees. But this was not the Kreuzerkrieg envisioned earlier by the Kaiser and Hollmann; it was the innovative deployment of U-boats as underwater commerce raiders, particularly in the unrestricted U-boat campaign of 1917. The *Handelskrieg* (literally "commerce war") campaign waged by the Kaiserliche Marine's U-boats resulted in the loss of over 12,500,000 tons of Allied and neutral shipping; in April 1917 alone U-boats sank 881,027 tons. Only the institution of convoys by the Royal Navy in late 1917 and the Kaiserliche Marine's lack of sufficient numbers of U-boats to maintain its advantage prevented Britain from facing a starvation blockade of its own.

G

SEEADLER

Deception proved to be *Seeadler*'s primary weapon. *Seeadler* had been disguised as a Norwegian windjammer, named *Hero*, with 29 out of the 64 crew being Norwegian speakers; Korvettenkapitän Luckner's deception even went as far as having one of the crew dress as his "wife" in case they were searched by British blockading forces. This was a wise contingency, for on Christmas Day 1916 *Seeadler* was stopped by the British armed merchant cruiser *Avenger* 185 miles south of Iceland but the boarding party found nothing suspicious about the "Norwegian" vessel. Luckner's method of capture was to approach Allied vessels (during the cruise Luckner had "Norge" and Norwegian flags painted on the side of the ship to add to the *ruse de guerre*) and signal them with a greeting, requesting news about the war, or with a request for a chronometer reading until the enemy was within gunnery range; at that point any Norwegian markings were covered over with sheets of canvas and *Seeadler* ran up the German ensign.

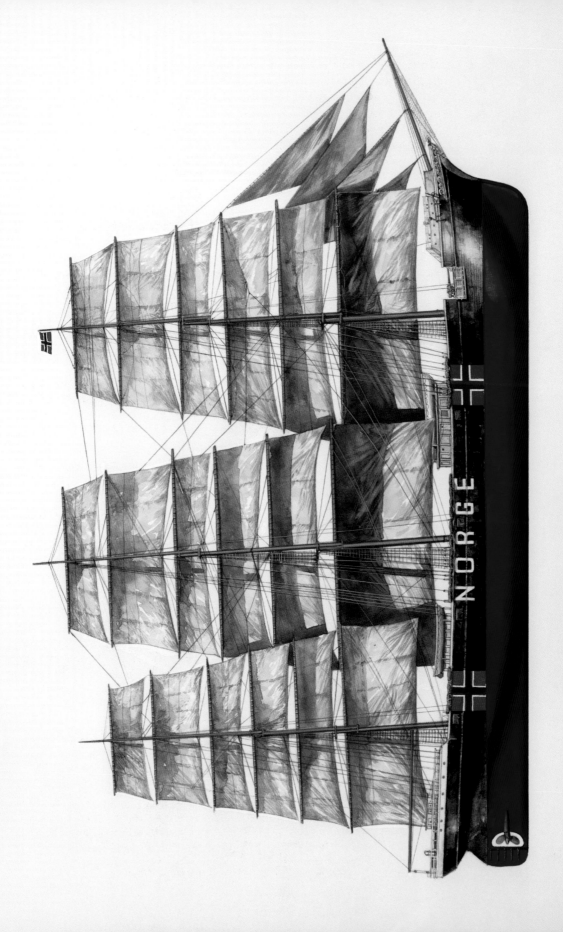

Wolf anchored alongside dreadnoughts of the High Seas Fleet in Kiel following her return. The successful cruises of *Möwe* and *Wolf* inspired the Kriegsmarine of the Third Reich to commission several Frachtdampfer-Hilfskreuzer during World War II.

Critics of the Kreuzerkrieg point to the disparity in tonnage losses inflicted by the U-boats and the surface raiders to argue that the results of the surface campaign did not justify its expense. German surface raiders sank a total of 162 Allied and neutral merchantmen and warships totaling 661,915 tons, or roughly 5 percent of the losses inflicted by U-boats. Nevertheless, when the surface raiders were at sea they did tie down substantial numbers of Allied warships and crews, resulting in resources having to be diverted from other fronts. Furthermore the propaganda value of the Kreuzerkrieg cannot be measured in terms of tonnage; particularly in the first year of the war their presence alone caused panic among British shipping lines, resulting in delays and shortages of goods at times as well as inflated maritime insurance rates (having a greater effect after the war in terms of a substantial addition to the overall wartime debt). Finally, the fact that the postwar Reichsmarine and Kriegsmarine of the Weimar Republic and the Third Reich renewed the strategy of Kreuzerkrieg in its prewar planning and building programs attests to the peripheral successes brought about by the surface raiders in World War I. The sheer presence and occasional raiding cruises conducted by the Kriegsmarine's battleships, *Panzerschiffe* ("armored ships," commonly known as pocket battleships), and heavy cruisers caused the Royal Navy a considerable amount of angst and tied down a disproportionate number of vessels. The successes of the Frachtdampfer-Hilfskreuzer, particularly *Möwe* and *Wolf* which together accounted for roughly half of the tonnage sunk in the Kreuzerkrieg, was not lost on the Kriegsmarine's strategists either. During 1940–1943, ten freighter-auxiliary cruisers deployed by the Kriegsmarine sank 118 Allied and neutral vessels totaling 736,929 tons.

BIBLIOGRAPHY

Beer, Karl-Theo, and Helmut Debelius. *S.M.S. Emden*. Herford: Koehlers Verlagsgesellschaft mbH, 1992.

Burdick, Charles. *The Frustrated Raider: The Story of the German Cruiser* Cormoran *in World War I*. Carbondale: Southern Illinois University Press, 1979.

Chesneau, Roger, and Eugène M. Kolesnik. *Conway's All the World's Fighting Ships, 1860–1905*. London: Conway Maritime Press, 1979.

Churchill, Winston Spencer. *The World Crisis, 1916–1918*. Vol. 2. New York: Charles Scribner's Sons, 1927.

Drechsel, Edwin. *Norddeutscher Lloyd Bremen, 1857–1970: History – Fleet – Ship Mails*. 2 volumes. Vancouver: Cordillera Publishing Company, 1995.

Farwell, Byron. *The Great War in Africa 1914–1918*. New York: W. W. Norton & Company, 1986.

Friedman, Norman. *Naval Weapons of World War One*. Barnsley: Seaforth Publishing, 2011.

Gardiner, Robert, and Randal Gray. *Conway's All the World's Fighting Ships, 1906–1921*. London: Conway Maritime Press, 1985.

Gottschall, Terrell D. *By Order of the Kaiser: Otto von Diederichs and the Rise of the Imperial German Navy, 1865–1902*. Annapolis: Naval Institute Press, 2003.

Guilliatt, Richard, and Peter Hohnen. *The Wolf: How One German Raider Terrorized the Allies in the Most Epic Voyage of WWI*. New York: Free Press, 2010.

Halpern, Paul G. *A Naval History of World War I*. London: UCL Press, 1994.

Herwig, Holger H. "The Failure of German Sea Power, 1914–1945: Mahan, Tirpitz, and Raeder Reconsidered." *The International History Review*, Vol. 10, No. 1 (Feb., 1988): 68–105.

Herwig, Holger H. *"Luxury" Fleet: The Imperial German Navy 1888–1918*. London: George Allen & Unwin, 1980.

Hoyt, Edwin P., Jr. *The Elusive Seagull: The Adventures of the World War One German Minelayer, the* Moewe. London: Leslie Frewin, 1970.

Kennedy, P. M. "The Development of German Naval Operations. Plans against England, 1896–1914." *The English Historical Review*, Vol. 89, No. 350 (1974): 48–76.

Lambi, Ivo Nikolai. *The Navy and German Power Politics, 1862–1914*. Boston: Allen & Unwin, 1984.

Lundeberg, Philip K. "The German Naval Critique of the U-Boat Campaign, 1915–1918." *Military Affairs*, Vol. 27, No. 3 (1963): 105–18.

Marder, Arthur J. *From the Dreadnought to Scapa Flow: The Royal Navy in the Fisher Era, 1904–1919*. 2 volumes. London: Oxford University Press, 1965.

Marrero, Javier Ponce. "Logistics for Commerce War in the Atlantic during the First World War: The German *Etappe* System in Action." *The Mariner's Mirror*, Vol. 92, No. 4 (Nov., 2006): 455–64.

Massie, Robert K. *Dreadnought: Britain, Germany, and the Coming of the Great War*. New York: Random House, 1991.

Overlack, Peter. "The Force of Circumstance: Graf Spee's Options for the East Asian Cruiser Squadron in 1914." *The Journal of Military History*, Vol. 60, No. 4 (Oct., 1996): 657–82.

Pardoe, Blaine. *The Cruise of the Sea Eagle: The Amazing True Story of Imperial Germany's Gentleman Pirate*. Manchester: Crécy Publishing Limited, 2009.

Putnam, William Lowell. *The Kaiser's Merchant Ships in World War I*. Jefferson: McFarland & Company, Inc., Publishers, 2001.

Raeder, Erich and Eberhard von Mantey. *Der Kreuzerkrieg in dem ausländischen Gewässern*. 3 volumes. Berlin: E. S. Mittler & Sohn, 1922–1937.

Schmalenbach, Paul. *German Raiders: A History of Auxiliary Cruisers of the German Navy, 1895–1945*. Annapolis: Naval Institute Press, 1979.

Steinberg, Jonathan. *Yesterday's Deterrent: Tirpitz and the Birth of the German Battle Fleet*. New York: The Macmillan Company, 1965.

Waldeyer-Hartz, Hugo von. *Der Kreuzerkrieg 1914–1918: Das Kreuzergeschwader*, Emden, Königsberg, Karlsruhe, *Die Hilfskreuzer*. Oldenburg: Gerhard Stalling, 1931.

Walter, John. *The Kaiser's Pirates: German Surface Raiders in World War One*. Annapolis: Naval Institute Press, 1994.

Wegener, Vizeadmiral Wolfgang. *Die Seestrategie des Weltkrieges*. Berlin: E. S. Mittler & Sohn, 1929.

Weir, Gary E. *Building the Kaiser's Navy: The Imperial Navy Office and German Industry in the von Tirpitz Era, 1890–1919*. Annapolis: Naval Institute Press, 1992.

Weir, Gary E. "Tirpitz, Technology, and Building U-boats, 1897–1916." *The International History Review*, Vol. 6, No. 2 (May, 1984): 174–90.

Yates, Keith. *Graf Spee's Raiders: Challenge to the Royal Navy, 1914–1915*. Annapolis: Naval Institute Press, 1995.

INDEX

Figures in **bold** refer to illustrations.